THE BHAGVAD GITA

M. K. GANDHI

adhyaya
BOOK'S HOUSE

Published by

ADHYAYA BOOKS HOUSE,

International Youth Club H-294, Plot 2A, First floor, Kehar Singh Estate,

Saidulajab, Lane No.2 Saket, New Delhi - 110030

Ph : +91 72762 00890

E-mail : adhyaya.bks@gmail.com

Edition : 2021

ISBN : 9789394178304

Published by Adhyaya Books House LLP.

Mohandas Karamchand Gandhi, or the Mahatama, was the leader of the Indian national movement. He fought the colonial regime with his philosophy of **Satyagraha** and **Ahimsa**. His birthday, October 2nd, is celebrated as the **International Day of Non-violence**

CONTENTS

FORWARD

The following pages by Mahadev Desai are an ambitious project. It represents his unremitting labours during his prison life in 1933-'34. Every page is evidence of his scholarship and exhaustive study of all he could lay hands upon regarding the Bhagavad Gita, poetically called the **Song Celestial** by Sir Edwin Arnold. The immediate cause of this labour of love was my translation in Gujarati of the divine book as I understood it. In trying to give a translation of my meaning of the Gita, he found himself writing an original commentary on the Gita.

The book might have been published during his lifetime, if I could have made time to go through the manuscript. I read some portions with him, but exigencies of my work had to interrupt the reading. Then followed the imprisonments of August 1942, and his sudden death within six days of our imprisonment. All of his immediate friends decided to give his reverent study of the Gita to the public. He had copies typed for his English friends who were impatient to see the commentary in print. And Pyarelal, who was collaborator with Mahadev Desai for many years, went through the whole manuscript and undertook to perform the difficult task of proof reading. Hence this publication.

Frankly, I do not pretend to any scholarship. I have, therefore, contended myself with showing the genesis of Mahadev Desai's effort. In so far as the translation part of the volume is concerned, I can vouch for its accuracy. He carried out the meaning of the original translation. I may add too that Pyarelal has interfered with the original only and in rare cases where it was considered to be essential, an interference which Mahadev Desai would, in my opinion, have gladly accepted, had he been alive.

On the train to Madras

M.K. GANDHI

20th January, 1946

INTRODUCTION

[It was at Kosani in Almora on 24th June, 1929, i.e., after two years' waiting, that I finished the introduction to my translation of the Gita. The whole was then published in due course. It has been translated in Hindi, Bengali and Marathi. There has been an insistent demand for an English translation. I finished the translation of the introduction at the Yeravda prison. Since my discharge it has lain with friends and now I give it to the reader. Those, who take no interest in the Book of Life, will forgive the trespass on these columns.* To those who are interested in the poem and treat it as their guide in life, my humble attempt might prove of some help.--M.K.G.]

(This translation appeared in the columns of the **Young India**, 6-8-1931, from where it has been reproduced here.)

I

Just as, acted upon by the affection of co-workers like Swami Anand and others, I wrote My Experiments with Truth, so has it been regarding my rendering of the Gita. "We shall be able to appreciate your meaning of the message of the Gita, only when we are able to study a translation of the whole text by yourself, with the addition of such notes as you may deem necessary. I do not think it is just on your part to deduce ahimsa etc. from stray verses," thus spoke Swami Anand to me during the non-cooperation days. I felt the force of his remarks. I, therefore, told him that I would adopt his suggestion when I got the time. Shortly afterwards I was imprisoned. During my incarceration I was able to study the Gita more fully. I went reverently through the Gujarati translation of the Lokamanya's great work. He had kindly presented me with the Marathi original and the translations in Gujarati and Hindi, and had asked me, if I could not tackle the original, at least to go through the Gujarati translation. I had not been able to follow the advice outside the prison walls. But when I was imprisoned I read the Gujarati translation. This reading whetted my appetite for more and I glanced through several works on the Gita.

My first acquaintance with the Gita began in 1888-89 with the verse translation by Sir Edwin Arnold known as the Song Celestial. On reading it, I felt a keen desire to read a Gujarati translation. And I read as many translations as I could lay hold of. But all such reading can give me no passport for presenting my own translation. Then again my knowledge of Sanskrit is limited, my knowledge of Gujarati too is in no way scholarly. How could I then dare present the public with my translation?

It has been my endeavor, as also that of some companions, to reduce to practice the teaching of the Gita as I have understood it. The Gita has become for us a spiritual reference book. I am aware that we ever fail to act in perfect accord with the teaching. The failure is not due to want of effort, but is in spite of it. Even though the failures we seem to see rays of hope. The accompanying rendering contains the meaning of the Gita message which this little band is trying to enforce in its daily conduct.

Again this rendering is designed for women, the commercial class, the so-called Shudras and the like who have little or no literary equipment, who have neither the time nor the desire to read the Gita in the original and yet who stand in need of its support. In spite of my Gujarati being unscholarly, I must own to having the desire to leave to the Gujaratis, through the mother tongue, whatever knowledge I may possess. I do indeed wish that at a time when literary output of a questionable character is pouring upon the Gujaratis, they should have before them a rendering the majority can understand of a book that is regarded as unrivalled for its spiritual merit and so withstand the overwhelming flood of unclean literature.

This desire does not mean any disrespect to the other renderings. They have their own place. But I am not aware of the claim made by the translators of enforcing their meaning of the Gita in their own lives. At the back of my reading there is the claim of an endeavour to enforce the meaning in my own conduct for an unbroken period of forty years. For this reason I do indeed harbour the wish that all Gujarati men or women wishing to shape their conduct according to their faith, should digest and derive strength from the translation here presented.

My co-workers, too, have worked at this translation. My knowledge of Sanskrit being very limited, I should not have full confidence in my literal translation. To that extent, therefore, the translation has passed before the eyes of Vinoba, Kaka Kalelkar, Mahadev Desai and Kishorlal Mashruwala.

II

Now about the message of the Gita.

Even in 1888-89, when I first became acquainted with the Gita, I felt that it was not a historical work, but that, under the guise of physical warfare, it described the duel that perpetually went on in the hearts mankind, and that physical warfare was brought in merely to make the description of the internal duel more alluring. This preliminary intuition became more confirmed on a closer study of religion and the Gita. A study of the Mahabharata gave it added confirmation. I do not regard the Mahabharata as a historical work in the accepted sense. The Adiparva contains powerful evidence in support of my opinion. By ascribing to the chief actors superhuman or subhuman origins, the great Vyasa made short work the history of kings and their peoples. The persons therein described may be historical, but the author of the Mahabharata has used them merely to drive home his religious theme.

The author of the Mahabharata has not established the necessity of physical warfare; on the contrary he has proved its futility. He has made the victors shed tears of sorrow and repentance, and has left them nothing but a legacy of miseries.

In this great work the Gita is the crown. Its second chapter, instead of teaching the rules of physical warfare, tells us how a perfected man is to be known. In the characteristics of the perfected man of the Gita, I do not see any to correspond to physical warfare. Its whole design is inconsistent with the rules of conduct governing the relations between warring parties.

Krishna of the Gita is perfection and right knowledge personified; but the picture is imaginary. That does not mean that Krishna, the adored of his people, never lived. But perfection is imagined. The idea of a perfect incarnation is an aftergrowth.

In Hinduism, incarnation is ascribed to one who has performed some extraordinary service of mankind. All embodied life is in reality an incarnation of God, but it is not usual to consider every living being an incarnation. Future generations pay this homage to one who, in his own generation, has been extraordinarily religious in his conduct. I can see nothing wrong in this procedure; it takes nothing from God's greatness, and there is no violence done to Truth. There is an Urdu saying which means, "Adam is not God but he is a spark of the Divine." And therefore he who is the most religiously behaved has most of the divine spark in him. It is in accordance with this train of thought that Krishna enjoys, in Hinduism, the status of the most perfect incarnation.

This belief in incarnation is a testimony of man's lofty spiritual ambition. Man is not at peace with himself til he has become like unto God. The endeavour to reach this state is the supreme, the only ambition worth having. And this is self-realization. This self-realization is the subject of the Gita, as it is of all scriptures. But its author surely did not write it to establish that doctrine. The object of the Gita appears to me to be that of showing the most excellent way to attain self-realization. That which is to be found, more or less clearly, spread out here and there in Hindu religious books, has been brought out in the clearest possible language in the Gita even at the risk of repetition.

That matchless remedy is renunciation of fruits of action.

This is the centre round which the Gita is woven. This renunciation is the central sun, round which devotion, knowledge and the rest revolve like planets. The body has been likened to a prison. There must be action where there is body. Not one embodied being is exempted from labour. And yet all religions proclaim that it is possible for man, by treating the body as the temple of God, to attain freedom. Every action is tainted, be it ever so trivial. How can the body be made the temple of God? In other words how can one be free from action, i.e. from the taint of sin? The Gita has answered the question in decisive language: "By desireless action; by renouncing fruits of action; by dedicating all activities to God, i.e., by surrendering oneself to Him body and soul."

But desirelessness or renunciation does not come for the mere talking about it. It is not attained by intellectual feat. It is attainable only by a constant heart-churn. Right knowledge is necessary for attaining renunciation. Learned men possess a knowledge of a kind. They may recite the Vedas from memory, yet they may be steeped in self-indulgence. In order that knowledge may not run riot, the author of the Gita has insisted on devotion accompanying it and has given it the first place. Knowledge without devotion will be like a misfire. Therefore, says the Gita, "Have devotion, and knowledge will follow." This devotion is not mere lip worship, it is a wrestling with death. Hence, the Gita's assessment of the devotee's quality is similar to that of the sage.

Thus the devotion required by the Gita is no soft-hearted effusiveness. It certainly is not blind faith. The devotion of the Gita has the least to do with the externals. A devotee may use, if he likes, rosaries, forehead marks, make offerings, but these things are no test of his devotion. He is the devotee who is jealous of none, who is a fount of mercy, who is without egotism, who is selfless, who treats alike cold and heat, happiness and misery, who is ever forgiving, who is always contented, whose resolutions are firm, who has dedicated mind and soul to God, who causes no dread, who is not afraid of others, who is free from exultation, sorrow and fear, who is pure, who is versed in action and yet remains unaffected by it, who renounces all fruit, good or bad, who treats friend and foe alike, who is untouched by respect or disrespect, who is not puffed up by praise, who does not go under when people speak ill of him who loves silence and solitude, who has a disciplined reason. Such devotion is inconsistent with the existence at the same time of strong attachments.

We thus see that to be a real devotee is to realize oneself. Self-realization is not something apart. One rupee can purchase for us poison or nectar, but knowledge or devotion cannot buy us salvation or bondage. These are not media of exchange. They are themselves the thing we want. In other words, if the means and the end are not identical, they are almost so. The extreme of means is salvation. Salvation of the Gita is perfect peace.

But such knowledge and devotion, to be true, have to stand the test of renunciation of fruits of action. Mere knowledge of right and wrong will not make one fit for salvation. According to common notions, a mere learned man will pass as a pandit. He need not perform any service. He will regard as bondage even to lift a little lota. Where one test of knowledge is non-liability for service, there is no room for such mundane work as the lifting of a lota.

Or take bhakti. The popular notion of bhakti is soft-heartedness, telling beads and the like, and disdaining to do even a loving service, least the telling of beads etc. might be interrupted. This bhakti, therefore, leaves the rosary only for eating, drinking and the like, never for grinding corn or nursing patients.

But the Gita says: No one has attained his goal without action. Even men like Janaka attained salvation through action. If even I were lazily to cease working, the world would not perish. How much more necessary then for the people at large to engage in action.

While on the one hand it is beyond dispute that all action binds, on the other hand it is equally true that all living beings have to do some work, whether they will or no. Here all activity, whether mental or physical is to be included in the term action. Then how is one to be free from the bondage of action, even though he may be acting? The manner in which the Gita has solved the problem is to my knowledge unique. The Gita says: 'Do your allotted work but renounce its fruit--be detached and work--have no desire for reward and work.'

This is the unmistakable teaching of the Gita. He who gives up action falls. He who gives up only the reward rises. But renunciation of fruit in no way means indifference to the result. In regard to every action one must know the result that is expected to follow, the means thereto, and the capacity for it. He, who, being thus equipped, is without desire for the result and is yet wholly engrossed in the due fulfillment of the task before him is said to have renounced the fruits of his action.

Again let no one consider renunciation to mean want of fruit for the renouncer. The Gita reading does not warrant such a meaning. Renunciation means absence of hankering after fruit. As a matter of fact, he who renounces reaps a thousandfold. The renunciation of the Gita is the acid test of faith. He who is ever brooding over result often loses nerve in the performance of his duty. He becomes impatient and then gives vent to anger and begins to do unworthy things; he jumps from action to action never remaining faithful to any. He who broods over results is like a man given to objects of senses; he is ever distracted, he says goodbye to all scruples, everything is right in his estimation and he therefore resorts to means fair and foul to attain his end.

From the bitter experiences of desire for fruit the author of the Gita discovered the path of renunciation of fruit and put it before the world in a most convincing manner. The common belief is that religion is always opposed to material good. "One cannot act religiously in mercantile and such other matters. There is no place for religion in such pursuits; religion is only for attainment of salvation," we here many worldly-wise people say. In my opinion the author of the Gita has dispelled this delusion. He has drawn no line of demarcation between salvation and worldly pursuits. On the contrary he has shown that religion must rule even our worldly pursuits. I have felt that the Gita teaches us that what cannot be followed out in day-to-day practice cannot be called religion. Thus, according to the Gita, all acts that are incapable of being performed without attachment are taboo. This golden rule saves mankind from many a pitfall. According to this interpretation murder, lying, dissoluteness and the like must be regarded as sinful and therefore taboo. Man's life then becomes simple, and from that simpleness springs peace.

Thinking along these lines, I have felt that in trying to enforce in one's life the central teaching of the Gita, one is bound to follow Truth and ahimsa. When there is no desire for fruit, there is no temptation for untruth or himsa. Take any instance of untruth or violence, and it will be found that at its back was the desire to attain the cherished end. But it may be freely admitted that the Gita was not written to establish ahimsa.

It was an accepted and primary duty even before the Gita age. The Gita had to deliver the message of renunciation of fruit. This is clearly brought out as early as the second chapter.

But if the Gita believed in ahimsa or it was included in desirelessness, why did the author take a warlike illustration? When the Gita was written, although people believed in ahimsa, wars were not only not taboo, but nobody observed the contradiction between them and ahimsa.

In assessing the implications of renunciation of fruit, we are not required to probe the mind of the author of the Gita as to his limitations of ahimsa and the like. Because a poet puts a particular truth before the world, it does not necessarily follow that he has known or worked out all its great consequences or that having done so, he is able always to express them fully. In this perhaps lies the greatness of the poem and the poet. A poet's meaning is limitless. Like man, the meaning of great writings suffers evolution. On examining the history of languages, we noticed that the meaning of important words has changed or expanded. This is true of the Gita. The author has himself extended the meanings of some of the current words. We are able to discover this even on superficial examination. It is possible that, in the age prior to that of the Gita, offering of animals as sacrifice was permissible. But there is not a trace of it in the sacrifice in the Gita sense. In the Gita continuous concentration on God is the king of sacrifices. The third chapter seems to show that sacrifice chiefly means body-labour for service. The third and fourth chapters read together will use other meanings for sacrifice, but never animal-sacrifice. Similarly has the meaning of the word sannyasa undergone, in the Gita, a transformation. The sannyasa of the Gita will not tolerate complete cessation of all activity. The sannyasa of the Gita is all work and yet no work. Thus the author of the Gita, by extending meanings of words, has taught us to imitate him. Let it be granted, that according to the letter of the Gita it is possible to say that warfare is consistent with renunciation of fruit. But after forty years' unremitting endeavor fully to enforce the teaching of the Gita in my own life, I have in all humility felt that perfect renunciation is impossible without perfect observance of ahimsa in every shape and form.

The Gita is not an aphoristic work; it is a great religious poem. The deeper you dive into it, the richer the meanings you get. It being meant for the people at large, there is pleasing repetition. With every age the important words will carry new and expanding meanings. But its central teaching will never vary. The teacher is at liberty to extract from this treasure any meaning he likes so as to enable him to enforce in his life the central teaching.

Nor is the Gita a collection of Do's and Dont's. What is lawful for one may be unlawful for another. What may be permissible at one time, or in one place, may not be so at another time, and in another place. Desire for fruit is the only universal prohibition. Desirelessness is obligatory.

The Gita has sung the praises of Knowledge, but it is beyond the mere intellect; it is essentially addressed to the heart and capable of being understood by the heart. Therefore the Gita is not for those who have no faith. The author makes Krishna say:

"Do not entrust this treasure to him who is without sacrifice, without devotion, without the desire for this teaching and who denies Me. On the other hand, those who will give this precious treasure to My devotees will, by the fact of this service, assuredly reach me. And those who, being free from malice, will with faith absorb this teaching, shall, having attained freedom, live where people of true merit go after death.

DISCOURCE 1.

No knowledge is to be found without seeking, no tranquility without travail, no happiness except through tribulation. Every seeker has, at one time or another, to pass through a conflict of duties, a heart-churning.

Dhritarashtra Said:

1. Tell me, O Sanjaya, what my sons and Pandu's assembled, on battle intent, did on the field of Kuru, the field of duty.

The human body is the battlefield where the eternal duel between right and wrong goes on. Therefore it is capable of being turned into a gateway to Freedom. It is born in sin and becomes the seed-bed of sin. Hence it is also called the field of Kuru. The Kuravas represent the forces of Evil, the Pandavas the forces of Good. Who is there that has not experienced the daily conflict within himself between the forces of Evil and the forces of Good?

Sanjaya Said:

2. On seeing the Pandava's army drawn up in battle array, King Duryodhana approached Drona, the preceptor, and addressed him thus:

3. Behold, O preceptor, this mighty army of the sons of Pandu, set in array by the son of Drupada, thy wise disciple.

4. Here are brave bowmen, peers of Bhima and Arjuna in fighting: Yuyudhana and Virata, and the 'Maharatha' Drupada.

5. Dhrishtaketu, Chekitana, valorous Kashiraja, Purujit the Kuntibhoja, and Shaibya, chief among men;

6. Valiant Yudhamanyu, valorous Uttamaujas, Subhadra's son, and the sons of Draupadi--each one of them a 'Maharatha'.

7. Acquaint thyself now, O best of Brahmanas, with the distinguished among us. I mention for thy information, the names of the captains of my army.

8. Thy noble self, Bhishma, Karna, and Kripa, victorious in battle, Ashvatthaman, Vikarna, also Somadatta's son;

9. There is many another hero, known for his skill in wielding diverse weapons, pledged to lay down his life for my sake, and all adepts in war.

10. This our force, commanded by Bhishma, is all too inadequate; while theirs, commanded by Bhima, is quite adequate.

11. Therefore, let each of you, holding your appointed places, at every entrance, guard only Bhishma.

12. At this, the heroic grandsire, the grand old man of the Kurus, gave a loud lion's roar and blew his conch to hearten Duryodhana.

13. Thereupon, conches, drums, cymbals and trumpets were sounded all at once. Terrific was the noise.

14. Then Madhava and Pandava, standing in their great chariot yoked with white steeds, blew their divine conches.

15. Hrishikesha blew the Panchajanya and Dhananjaya the Devadatta; while the wolf-bellied Bhima of dread deeds sounded his great conch Paundra.

16. King Yudhishthira, Kunti's son, blew the Anantavijaya, and Nakula nd Sahadeva their conches, Sughosha and Manipushpaka.

17. And Kashiraja, the great bowman, Shikhandi the 'Maharatha', Dhrishtadyumna, Virata and Satyaki, the unconquerable;

18. Drupada, Draupadi's sons, the strong-armed son of Subhadra, all these, O King, blew each his own conch.

19. That terrifying tumult, causing earth and heaven to resound, rent the hearts of Dhritarashtra's sons.

20-21. Then, O King, the ape-bannered Pandava, seeing Dhritarashtra's sons arrayed and flight of arrows about to begin, took up his bow, and spoke thus to Hrishikesha: "Set my chariot between the two armies, O Achyuta!"

22. That I may behold them drawn up, on battle intent, and know whom I have to engage in this fearful combat;

23. And that I may survey the fighters assembled here anxious to fulfil in battle perverse Duryodhana's desire.

Sanjaya Said:

24-25. Thus addressed by Gudakesha, O King, Hrishikesha set the unique chariot between the two armies in front of Bhishma, Drona and all the kings and said: Behold, O Partha, the Kurus assembled yonder.

26-28. Then did Partha see, standing there, sires, grandsires, preceptors, uncles, brothers, sons, grandsons, comrades, fathers-in-law and friends in both armies. Beholding all these kinsmen ranged before him, Kaunteya was overcome with great compassion and spake thus in anguish:

Arjuna Said:

28-29. As I look upon these kinsmen, O Krishna, assembled here eager to fight, my limbs fail, my mouth is parched, a tremor shakes my frame and my hair stands on end.

30. Gandiva slips from my hand, my skin is on fire, I cannot keep my feet, and my mind reels.

31. I have unhappy forebodings, O Keshava; and I see no good in slaying kinsmen in battle.

32. I seek not victory, nor sovereign power, nor earthly joys. What good are sovereign power, worldly pleasures and even life to us, O Govinda?

33. Those for whom we would desire sovereign power, earthly joys and delights are here arrayed in battle, having renounced life and wealth--

34. Preceptors, sires, grandsires, sons and even grandsons, uncles, fathers-in-law, brothers-in-law, and other kinsmen.

35. These I would not kill, O Madhusudana, even though they slay me, not even for kingship of the three worlds, much less for an earthly kingdom.

36. What pleasure can there be in slaying these sons of Dhritarashtra, O Janardana? Sin only can be our lot, if we slay these, usurpers though they be.

37. It does not therefore behove us to kill our kinsmen, these sons of Dhritarashtra. How may we be happy, O Madhava, in killing our own kins?

38. Even though these, their wits warped by greed, see not the guilt that lies in destroying the family, nor the sin of treachery to comrades;

39. How can we, O Janardana, help recoiling from this sin, seeing clearly as we do the guilt that lies in such destruction?

40. With the destruction of the family perish the eternal family virtues, and with the perishing of these virtues unrighteousness seizes the whole family.

41. When unrighteousness prevails, O Krishna, the women of the family become corrupt, and their corruption, O Varshneya, causes a confusion of varnas.

42. This confusion verily drags the family-slayer, as well as the family, to hell, and for want of obsequial offerings and rites their departed sires fall from blessedness.

43. By the sins of these family-slayers resulting in confusion of varnas, the eternal tribal and family virtues are brought to naught.

44. For we have had it handed down to us, O Janardana, that the men whose family virtues have been ruined are doomed to dwell in hell.

45. Alas! What a heinous sin we are about to commit, in that, from greed of the joy of sovereign power, we are prepared to slay our kith and kin!

46. Happier far would it be for me if Dhritarashtra's sons, weapons in hand, should strike me down on the battlefield, unresisting and unarmed.

Sanjaya Said:

47. Thus spake Arjuna on the field of battle, and dropping his bow and arrows sank down on his seat in the chariot, overwhelmed with anguish.

Thus ends the first discourse, entitled 'Arjuna Vishada Yoga' in the converse of Lord Krishna and Arjuna, on the science of Yoga as part of the knowledge of Brahman in the Upanishad called the Bhagawadgita.

DISCOURCE 2.

By reason of delusion, man takes wrong to be right. By reason of delusion was Arjuna led to make a difference between kinsmen and non-kinsmen. To demonstrate that this is a vain distinction, Lord Krishna distinguishes between body (not-Self) and Atman (Self) and shows that whilst bodies are impermanent and several, Atman is permanent and one. Effort is within man's control, not the fruit thereof. All he has to do, therefore, is to decide his course of conduct or duty on each occasion and persevere in it, unconcerned about the result. Fulfillment of one's duty in the spirit of detachment or selflessness leads to Freedom.

Sanjaya Said:

1. To Arjuna, thus overcome with compassion, sorrowing, and his eyes obscured by flowing tears, Madhusudana spake these words:

The Lord Said:

2. How is it that at this perilous moment this delusion, unworthy of the noble, leading neither to heaven nor to glory, has overtaken thee?

3. Yield not to unmanliness, O Partha; it does not become thee. Shake off this miserable faint-heartedness and arise, O Parantapa!

Arjuna Said:

4. How shall I, with arrows, engage Bhishma and Drona in battle, O Madhusudana, they who are worthy of reverence, O Arisudana?

5. It were better far to live on alms of this world than to slay these venerable elders. Having slain them I should but have blood-stained enjoyments.

6. Nor do we know which is better for us, that we conquer them or that they conquer us, for here stand before us Dhritarashtra's sons having killed whom we should have no desire to live.

7. My being is paralysed by faint-heartedness; my mind discerns not duty; hence I ask thee; tell me, I pray thee, in no uncertain language, wherein lies my good. I am thy disciple; guide me; I see refuge in thee.

8. For I see nothing that can dispel the anguish that shrivels up my senses even if I should win on earth uncontested sovereignty over a thriving kingdom or lordship over the gods.

Sanjaya Said:

9. Thus spoke Gudakesha Parantapa to Hrishikesha Govinda, and with the words 'I will not fight' became speechless.

10. To him thus stricken with anguish, O Bharata! between the two armies, Hrishikesha, as though mocking, addressed these words:

The Lord Said:

11. Thou mournest for them whom thou shouldst not mourn and utterest vain words of wisdom. The wise mourn neither for the living nor for the dead.

12. For never was I not, nor thou, nor these kings; nor will any of us cease to be hereafter.

13. As the embodied one has, in the present body, infancy, youth and age, even so does he receive another body. The wise man is not

deceived therein.

14. O Kaunteya! contacts of the senses with their objects bring cold and heat, pleasure and pain; they come and go and are transient. Endure them, O Bharata.

15. O noblest of men, the wise man who is not disturbed by these, who is unmoved by pleasure and pain, he is fitted for immortality.

16. What is non-Being is never known to have been, and what is Being is never known not to have been. Of both these the secret has been seen by the seers of the Truth.

17. Know that to be imperishable whereby all this is pervaded. No one can destroy that immutable being.

18. These bodies of the embodied one who is eternal, imperishable and immeasurable are finite. Fight, therefore, O Bharata.

19. He who thinks of This (Atman) as slayer and he who believes This to be slain, are both ignorant. This neither slays nor is ever slain.

20. This is never born nor ever dies, nor having been will ever not be any more; unborn, eternal, everlasting, ancient, This is not slain when the body is slain.

21. He who knows This, O Partha, to be imperishable, eternal, unborn, and immutable—whom and how can that man slay or cause to be slain?

22. As a man casts off worn-out garments and takes others that are new, even so the embodied one casts off worn-out bodies and passes on to others new.

23. This no weapons wound, This no fire burns, This no waters wet, This no wind doth dry.

24. Beyond all cutting, burning, wetting and drying is This-eternal, all-pervading, stable, immovable, everlasting.

25. Perceivable neither by the senses nor by the mind, This is called unchangeable; therefore knowing This as such thou shouldst not grieve.

26. And if thou deemest This to be always coming to birth and always dying, even then, O Mahababu, thou shouldst not grieve.

27. For certain is the death of the born, and certain is the birth of the dead; therefore what is unavoidable thou shouldst not regret.

28. The state of all beings before birth is unmanifest; their middle state manifest; their state after death is again unmanifest. What occasion is there for lament, O Bharata?

29. One looks upon This as a marvel; another speaks of This as such; another hears thereof as a marvel; yet having heard This none truly knows This.

30. This embodied one in the body of every being is ever beyond all harm, O Bharata; thou shouldst not, therefore, grieve for any one.

Thus far Lord Krishna, by force of argument based on pure reason, has demonstrated that Atman is abiding while the physical body is fleeting, and has explained that if, under certain circumstances, the destruction of a physical body is deemed justifiable, it is delusion to imagine that the Kauravas should not be slain because they are kinsmen. Now he reminds Arjuna of the duty of a Kshatriya.

31. Again, seeing thine own duty thou shouldst not shrink from it; for there is no higher good for a Kshatriya than a righteous war.

32. Such a fight, coming unsought, as a gateway to heaven thrown open, falls only to the lot of happy Kshatriyas, O Partha.

33. But if thou wilt not fight this righteous fight, then failing in thy duty and losing thine honour thou wilt incur sin.

34. The world will for ever recount the story of thy disgrace; and for a man of honour disgrace is worse than death.

35. The Maharathas will think that fear made thee retire from battle; and thou wilt fall in the esteem of those very ones who have held thee high.

36. Thine enemies will deride thy prowess and speak many unspeakable words about thee. What can be more painful than that?

37. Slain, thou shalt gain heaven; victorious, thou shall inherit the earth: therefore arise, O Kaunteya, determined to fight.

Having declared the highest truth, viz. the immortality of the eternal Atman and the fleeting nature of the physical body (11-30), Krishna reminds Arjuna that a Kshatriya may not flinch from a fight which comes unsought (31-32). He then (33-37) shows how the highest truth and the performance of duty incidentally coincide with expediency. Next he proceeds to foreshadow the central teaching of the Gita in the following shloka.

38. Hold alike pleasure and pain, gain and loss, victory and defeat, and gird up thy loins for the fight; so doing thou shalt not incur sin.

39. Thus have I set before thee the attitude of Knowledge; hear now the attitude of Action; resorting to this attitude thou shalt cast off the bondage of action.

40. Here no effort undertaken is lost, no disaster befalls. Even a little of this righteous course delivers one from great fear.

41. The attitude, in this matter, springing, as it does, from fixed resolve is but one, O Kurunandana; but for those who have no fixed resolve the attitudes are many-branched and unending.

When the attitude ceases to be one and undivided and becomes many and divided, it ceases to be one settled will, and is broken up into various wills of desires between which man is tossed about.

42-44. The ignorant, revelling in the letter of the Vedas, declare that there is naught else; carnally-minded, holding heaven to be their goal, they utter swelling words which promise birth as the fruit of action and which dwell on the many and varied rites to be performed for the sake of pleasure and power; intent, as they are, on pleasure and power their swelling words rob them of their wits, and they have no settled attitude which can be centered on the supreme goal.

The Vedic ritual, as opposed to the doctrine of Yoga laid down in the Gita, is alluded to here. The Vedic ritual lays countless ceremonies and rites with a view to attaining merit and heaven. These, divorced as they are from the essence of the Vedas and short-lived in their result, are worthless.

45. The Vedas have as their domain the three gunas; eschew them, O Arjuna. Free thyself from the pairs of opposites, abide in eternal truth, scorn to gain or guard anything, remain the master of thy soul.

46. To the extent that a well is of use when there is a flood of water on all sides, to the same extent are all the Vedas of use to an enlightened Brahmana.

47. Action alone is thy province, never the fruits thereof; let not thy motive be the fruit of action, nor shouldst thou desire to avoid action.

48. Act thou, O Dhananjaya, without attachment, steadfast in Yoga, even-minded in success and failure. Even-mindedness is Yoga.

49. For action, O Dhananjaya, is far inferior to unattached action; seek refuge in the attitude of detached action. Pitiable are those who make fruit their motive.

50. Here in this world a man gifted with that attitude of detachment escapes the fruit of both good and evil deeds. Gird thyself up for Yoga, therefore. Yoga is skill in action.

51. For sages, gifted with the attitude of detachment, who renounce the fruit of action, are released from the bondage of birth and attain to the state which is free from all ills.

52. When thy understanding will have passed through the slough of delusion, then wilt thou be indifferent alike to what thou hast heard and wilt hear.

53. When thy understanding, distracted by much hearing, will rest steadfast and unmoved in concentration, then wilt thou attain Yoga.

Arjuna Said:

54. What, O Keshava, is the mark of the man whose understanding is secure, whose mind is fixed in concentration? How does he talk? How sit? How move.

The Lord Said:

55. When a man puts away, O partha, all the cravings that arise in the mind and finds comfort for himself only from Atman, then he is called the man of secure understanding.

To find comfort for oneself from Atman means to look to the spirit within for spiritual comfort, not to outside objects which in their very nature must give pleasure as well as pain. Spiritual comfort or bliss must be distinguished from pleasure or happiness. The pleasure I may derive from the possession of wealth, for instance, is delusive; real spiritual comfort or bliss can be attained only if I rise superior to every temptation even though troubled by the pangs of poverty and hunger.

56. Whose mind is untroubled in sorrows and longeth not for joys, who is free from passion, fear and wrath—he is called the ascetic of secure understanding.

57. Who owns attachment nowhere, who feels neither joy nor resentment whether good or bad comes his way—that man's understanding is secure.

58. And when, like the tortoise drawing in its limbs from every side, this man draws in his senses from their objects, his understanding is

secure.

59. When a man starves his senses, the objects of those senses disappear from him, but not the yearning for them; the yearning too departs when he beholds the Supreme.

The shloka does not rule out fasting and other forms of self-restraint, but indicates their limitations, these restraints are needed for subduing the desire for sense-objects, which however is rooted out only when one has a vision of the Supreme. The higher yearning conquers all the lower yearnings.

60. For, in spite of the wise man's endeavour, O Kaunteya, the unruly senses distract his mind perforce.

61. Holding all these in check, the yogi should sit intent on Me; for he whose senses are under control is secure of understanding.

This means that without devotion and the consequent grace of God, man's endeavour is vain.

62. In a man brooding on objects of the senses, attachment to them springs up; attachment begets craving and craving begets wrath.

Craving cannot but lead to resentment, for it is unending and unsatisfied.

63. Wrath breeds stupefaction, stupefaction leads to loss of memory, loss of memory ruins the reason, and the ruin of reason spells utter destruction.

64. But the disciplined soul, moving among sense-objects with the senses weaned from likes and dislikes and brought under the control of Atman, attains peace of mind.

65. Peace of mind means the end to all ills, for the understanding of him whose mind is at peace stands secure.

66. The undisciplined man has neither understanding nor devotion;

for him who has no devotion there is no peace, and for him who has no peace whence happiness?

67. For when his mind runs after any of the roaming senses, it sweeps away his understanding, as the wind a vessel upon the waters.

68. Therefore, O Mahabahu, he, whose senses are reined in on all sides from their objects, is the man of secure understanding.

69. When it is night for all other beings, the disciplined soul is awake; when all other beings are awake, it is night for the seeing ascetic.

This verse indicates the divergent paths of the discipline ascetic and sensual man. Whereas the ascetic is dead to the things of the world and lives in God, the sensual man is alive only to the things of the world and dead to the things of the spirit.

70. He in whom all longings subside, even as the waters subside in the ocean which, though ever being filled by them, never overflows—that man finds peace; not he who cherishes longing.

71. The man who sheds all longing and moves without concern, free from the sense of 'I' and 'Mine'—he attains peace.

72. This is the state, O partha, of the man who rests in Brahman; having attained to it, he is not deluded. He who abides in this state even at the hour of death passes into oneness with Brahman.

Thus ends the second discourse, entitled 'Sankhya Yoga' in the converse of Lord Krishna and Arjuna, on the science of Yoga as part of the knowledge of Brahman in the Upanishad called the Bhagawadgita.

DISCOURCE 3.

This discourse may be said to be the key to the essence of the Gita. It makes absolutely clear the spirit and the nature of right action and shows how true knowledge must express itself in acts of selfless service.

Arjuna Said:

1. If, O Janardana, thou holdest that the attitude of detachment is superior to action, then why, O Keshava, dost thou urge me to dreadful action?

2. Thou dost seem to confuse my understanding with perplexing speech; tell me, therefore, in no uncertain voice, that alone whereby I may attain salvation.

Arjuna is sore perplexed, for whilst on the one hand he is rebuked for his faint-heartedness, on the other he seems to be advised to refrain from action (II.49-50). But this, in reality, is not the case as the following shlokas will show.

The Lord Said:

3. I have spoken, before, O sinless one, of two attitudes in this world—the Sankhayas', that of Jnana yoga and the Yogins', that of karma yoga.

4. Never does man enjoy freedom from action by not undertaking

action, nor does he attain that freedom by mere renunciation of action.

'Freedom from action' is freedom from the bondage of action. This freedom is not to be gained by cessation of all activity, apart from the fact that this cessation is in the very nature of things impossible (see following shloka). How then may it be gained? The following shlokas will explain.

5. For none ever remains inactive even for a moment; for all are compelled to action by the gunas inherent in prakriti.

6. He who curbs the organs of action but allows the mind to dwell on the sense-objects,—such a one, wholly deluded, is called a hypocrite.

The man who curbs his tongue but mentally swears at another is a hypocrite. But that does not mean that free rein should be given to the organs of action so long as the mind cannot be brought under control. Self-imposed physical restraint is a condition precedent to mental restraint. Physical restraint should be entirely self-imposed and not super-imposed from outside, e.g. by fear. The hypocrite who is held up to contempt here is not the humble aspirant after self-restraint. The shloka has reference to the man who curbs the body because he cannot help it while indulging the mind, and who would indulge the body too if he possibly could. The next shloka puts the thing conversely.

7. But he, O Arjuna, who keeping all the senses under control of the mind, engages the organs in Karma yoga, without attachment—that man excels.

The mind and body should be made to accord well. Even with the mind kept in control, the body will be active in one way or another. But he whose mind is truly restrained will, for instance, close his ears to foul talk and open them only to listen to the praise of God or of good men. He will have no relish for sensual pleasures and will keep himself occupied with such activity as ennobles the soul. That is the path of action. Karma yoga is the yoga (means) which will deliver the self from the bondage of the body, and in it there is no room for self-indulgence.

8. Do thou thy allotted task; for action is superior to inaction; with inaction even life's normal course is not possible.

9. This world of men suffers bondage from all action save that which is done for the sake of sacrifice; to this end, O Kaunteya, perform action without attachment.

'Action for the sake of sacrifice' means acts of selfless service dedicated to God.

10. Together with sacrifice did the Lord of beings create, of old, mankind, declaring:

"By this shall ye increase; may this be to you the giver of all your desires.

11. "With this may you cherish the gods and may the gods cherish you; thus cherishing one another may you attain the highest good.

12. "Cherished with sacrifice, the gods will bestow on you the desired boons." He who enjoys their gifts without rendering aught unto them is verily a thief.

"Gods" in shlokas 11 and 12 must be taken to mean the whole creation of God. The service of all created beings is the service of the gods and the same is sacrifice.

13. The righteous men who eat the residue of the sacrifice are freed from all sin, but the wicked who cook for themselves eat sin.

14. From food springs all life, from rain is born food; from sacrifice comes rain and sacrifice is the result of action.

15. Know that action springs from Brahman and Brahman from the

Imperishable; hence the all-pervading Brahman is ever firm-founded on sacrifice.

16. He who does not follow the wheel thus set in motion here below, he, living in sin, sating his senses, lives, O Partha, in vain.

17. But the man who revels in Atman, who is content in Atman and who is satisfied only with Atman, for him no action exists.

18. He has no interest whatever in anything done, nor in anything not done, nor has he need to rely on anything for personal ends.

19. Therefore, do thou ever perform without attachment the work that thou must do; for performing action without attachment man attains the Supreme.

20. For through action alone Janaka and others achieved perfection; even with a view to the guidance of mankind thou must act.

21. Whatever the best man does, is also done by other men, what example he sets, the world follows.

22. For me, O Partha, there is naught to do in the three worlds, nothing worth gaining that I have not gained; yet I am ever in action.

An objection is sometimes raised that God being impersonal is not likely to perform any physical activity, at best He may be supposed to act mentally. This is not correct. For the unceasing movement of the sun, the moon, the earth etc. signifies God in action. This is not mental but physical activity. Though God is without form and impersonal, He acts as though He had form and body. Hence though He is ever in action, He is free from action, unaffected by action. What must be borne in mind is that, just as all Nature's movements and processes are mechanical and yet guided by Divine Intelligence or Will, even so man must reduce his daily conduct to mechanical regularity and precision, but he must do so intelligently. Man's merit lies in observing divine guidance at the back of these processes and in an intelligent imitation of it rather than in emphasizing the mechanical nature thereof and reducing himself to an automation. One has but to withdraw the self, withdraw attachment to fruit from all action, and then not only mechanical precision but security from all wear and tear will be ensured. Acting thus man remains fresh until the end of his days. His body will perish in due course, but his soul will remain evergreen without a crease or a wrinkle.

23. Indeed, for were I not, unslumbering, ever to remain in action, O Partha, men would follow my example in every way.

24. If I were not to perform my task, these worlds would be ruined; I should be the same cause of chaos and of the end of all mankind.

25. Just as, with attachment, the unenlightened perform all actions, O Bharata, even so, but unattached, should the enlightened man act, with a desire for the welfare of humanity.

26. The enlightened may not confuse the mind of the unenlightened, who are attached to action; rather must he perform all actions unattached, and thus encourage them to do likewise.

27. All action is entirely done by the gunas of prakriti. Man, deluded by the sense of 'I', thinks, 'I am the doer'.

28. But he, O Mahabahu, who understands the truth of the various gunas and their various activities, knows that it is the gunas that operate on the gunas; he does not claim to be the doer.

As breathing, winking and similar processes are automatic and man claims no agency for them, he being conscious of the processes only when disease or similar cause arrests them, in a similar manner all his acclivities should be automatic, without his arrogating to himself the agency or responsibility thereof. A man of charity does not even know that he is doing charitable acts, it is his nature to do so, he cannot help it. This detachment can only come from tireless endeavour and God's grace.

29. Deluded by the gunas of prakriti men become attached to the

activities of the gunas; he who knows the truth of things should not unhinge the slow-witted who have not the knowledge.

30. Cast all thy acts on Me, with thy mind fixed on the indwelling Atman, and without any thought of fruit, or sense of 'mine' shake off thy fever and fight!

He who knows the Atman inhabiting the body and realizes Him to be a part of the supreme Atman will dedicate everything to Him, even as a faithful servant acts as a mere shadow of his master and dedicates to him all that he does. For the master is the real doer, the servant but the instrument.

31. Those who always act according to the rule I have here laid down, in faith and without cavilling—they too are released from the bondage of their actions.

32. But those who cavil at the rule and refuse to conform to it are fools, dead to all knowledge; know that they are lost.

33. Even a man of knowledge acts according to his nature; all creatures follow their nature; what then will constraint avail?

This does not run counter to the teaching in II. 61 and II. 68. Self-restraint is the means of salvation (VI. 35; XIII. 7). Man's energies should be bent towards achieving complete self-restraint until the end of his days. But if he does not succeed, neither will constraint help him. The shloka does not rule out restraint but explains that nature prevails. He who justifies himself saying, 'I cannot do this, it is not in my nature,' misreads the shloka. True we do not know our nature, but habit is not nature. Progress, not decline, ascent, not descent, is the nature of the soul, and therefore every threatened decline or descent ought to be resisted. The next verse makes this abundantly clear.

34. Each sense has its settled likes and dislikes towards its objects; man should not come under the sway of these, for they are his

besetters.

Hearing, for instance, is the object of the ears which may be inclined to hear something and disinclined to hear something else. Man may not allow himself to be swayed by these likes and dislikes, but must decide for himself what is conducive to his growth, his ultimate end being to reach the state beyond happiness and misery.

35. Better one's own duty, bereft of merit, than another's well-performed; better is death in the discharge of one's duty; another's duty is fraught with danger.

One man's duty may be to serve the community by working as a sweeper, another's may be to work as an accountant. An accountant's work may be more inviting, but that need not draw the sweeper away from his work.

Should he allow himself to be drawn away he would himself be lost and put the community into danger. Before God the work of man will be judged by the spirit in which it is done, not by the nature of the work which makes no difference whatsoever. Whoever acts in a spirit of dedication fits himself for salvation.

Arjuna Said:

36. Then what impels man to sin, O Varshneya, even against his will, as though by force compelled?

The Lord Said:

37. It is Lust, it is Wrath, born of the guna—Rajas. It is the arch-devourer, the arch-sinner. Know this to be man's enemy here.

38. As fire is obscured by smoke, a mirror by dirt, and the embryo by the amnion, so is knowledge obscured by this.

39. Knowledge is obscured, O Kaunteya, by this eternal enemy of the wise man, in the form of Lust, the insatiable fire.

40. The senses, the mind and the reason are said to be its great seat; by means of these it obscures knowledge and stupefies man.

When Lust seizes the senses, the mind is corrupted, discrimination is obscured and reason ruined. See II. 62-64.

41. Therefore, O Bharatarshabha, bridle thou first the senses and then rid thyself of this sinner, the destroyer of knowledge and discrimination.

42. Subtle, they say, are the senses; subtler than the senses is the mind; subtler than the mind is the reason; but subtler even than the reason is He.

43. Thus realizing Him to be subtler than the reason, and controlling the self by the Self (Atman), destroy, O Mahabahu, this enemy—Lust, so hard to overcome.

When man realizes Him, his mind will be under his control, not swayed by the senses. And when the mind is conquered, what power has Lust? It is indeed a subtle enemy, but when once the senses, the mind and the reason are under the control of the subtlemost Self, Lust is extinguished.

Thus ends the third discourse entitled 'Karma Yoga' in the converse of Lord Krishna and Arjuna, on the science of Yoga, as part of the knowledge of Brahman in the Upanishad called the Bhagawadgita.

DISCOURCE 4.

This discourse further explains the subject-matter of the third and describes the various kinds of sacrifice.

The Lord Said:

1. I expounded this imperishable yoga to Vivasvat; Vivasvat communicated it to Manu, and Manu to Ikshvaku.

2. Thus handed down in succession, the royal sages learnt it; with long lapse of time it dwindled away in this world, O Parantapa.

3. The same ancient yoga have I expounded to thee today; for thou art My devotee and My friend, and this is the supreme mystery.

Arjuna Said:

4. Later was Thy birth, my Lord, earlier that of Vivasvat. How then am I to understand that Thou didst expound it in the beginning?

The Lord Said:

5. Many births have we passed through, O Arjuna, both thou and I; I know them all, thou knowest them not, O Parantapa.

Though unborn and inexhaustible in My essence, though Lord of all beings, yet assuming control over My Nature, I come into being by My mysterious power.

7. For whenever Right declines and Wrong prevails, then O Bharata, I come to birth.

8. To save the righteous, to destroy the wicked, and to re-establish Right I am born from age to age.

Here is comfort for the faithful and affirmation of the truth that Right ever prevails. An eternal conflict between Right and Wrong goes on. Sometimes the latter seems to get the upper hand, but it is Right which ultimately prevails. The good are never destroyed, for Right—which is Truth—cannot perish; the wicked are destroyed, because Wrong has no independent existence. Knowing this let man cease to arrogate to himself authorship and eschew untruth, violence and evil. Inscrutable Providence—the unique power of the Lord—is ever at work. This in fact is avatara, incarnation. Strictly speaking there can be no birth for God.

9. He who knows the secret of this My divine birth and action is not born again, after leaving the body; he comes to Me, O Arjuna.

For when a man is secure in the faith that Right always prevails, he never swerves therefrom, pursuing to the bitterest end and against serious odds, and as no part of the effort proceeds from his ego, but all is dedicated to Him, being ever one with Him, he is released from birth to death.

10. Freed from passion, fear and wrath, filled full with Me, relying on Me, and refined by the fiery ordeal of knowledge, many have become one with Me.

11. In whatever way men resort to Me, even so do I render to them. In every way, O Partha, the path men follow is Mine.

That is, the whole world is under His ordinance. No one may break God's law with impunity. As we sow, so shall we reap. This law operates inexorably without fear or favor.

12. Those who desire their actions to bear fruit worship the gods

here; for in this world of men the fruit of action is quickly obtainable.

Gods, as indicated before, must not be taken to mean the heavenly beings of tradition, but whatever reflects the divine. In that sense man is also a god. Steam, electricity and the other great forces of Nature are all gods. Propitiation of these forces quickly bears fruit, as we well know, but it is short-lived. It fails to bring comfort to the soul and it certainly does not take one even a short step towards salvation.

13. The order of the four varnas was created by Me according to the different gunas and karma of each; yet know that though, therefore, author thereof, being changeless I am not the author.

14. Actions do not affect Me, nor am I concerned with the fruits thereof. He who recognizes Me as such is not bound by actions.

For man has thus before him the supreme example of one who though in action is not the doer thereof. And when we are but instruments in His hands, where then is the room for arrogating responsibility for action?

15. Knowing this did men of old, desirous of freedom, perform action; do thou, then, just as they did—the men of old in days gone by.

16. 'What is action? What is inaction?'—here even the wise are perplexed. I will then expound to thee that action knowing which thou shalt be saved from evil.

17. For it is meet to know the meaning of action, of forbidden action, as also inaction. Impenetrable is the secret of action.

18. Who sees action in action and action in inaction, he is enlightened among men, he is a yogi, he has done all he need do.

The 'action' of him who, though ever active, does not claim to be the doer, is inaction; and the 'inaction' of him who, though outwardly avoiding action, is always building castles in his own mind, is action. The enlightened man who has grasped the secret of action knows that no action proceeds from him, all proceeds from God and hence he selflessly remains absorbed in action. He is the true yogi. The man who acts self-fully misses the secret of action and cannot distinguish between Right and Wrong. The soul's natural progress is towards selflessness and purity and one might, therefore, say that the man who strays from the path of purity strays from selflessness. All actions of the selfless man are naturally pure.

19. He whose every undertaking is free from desire and selfish purpose, and he who has burnt all his actions in the fire of knowledge—such an one the wise call a pandita.

20. He who has renounced attachment to the fruit of action, who is ever content, and free from all dependence,—he, though immersed in action, yet acts not.

That is, his action does not bind him.

21. Expecting naught, holding his mind and body in check, putting away every possession, and going through action only in the body he incurs no stain.

The purest act, if tainted by 'self', binds. But when it is done in a spirit of dedication, it ceases to bind. When 'self' has completely subsided, it is only the body that works. For instance, in the case of a man who is asleep his body alone is working. A prisoner doing his prison tasks has surrendered his body to the prison authorities and only his body, therefore, works. Similarly, he who has voluntarily made himself God's prisoner, does nothing himself. His body mechanically acts, the doer is God, hot he. He has reduced himself to nothingness.

22. Content with whatever chance may bring, rid of the pairs of opposites, free from ill-will, even-minded in success and failure, he is not bound though he acts.

23. Of the free soul who has shred all attachment, whose mind is firmly grounded in knowledge, who acts only for sacrifice, all karma is extinguished.

24. The offering of sacrifice is Brahman; the oblation is Brahman; it is offered by Brahman in the fire that is Brahman; thus he whose mind is fixed on acts dedicated to Brahman must needs pass on to Brahman.

25. Some yogins perform sacrifice in the form of worship of the gods, others offer sacrifice of sacrifice itself in the fire that is Brahman.

26. Some offer as sacrifice the sense of hearing and the other senses in the fires of restraint; others sacrifice sound and the other objects of sense in the fires of the senses.

The restraint of the senses—hearing and others—is one thing; and directing them only to legitimate objects, e.g. listening to hymns in the praise of god, is another, although ultimately both amount to the same thing.

27. Others again sacrifice all the activities of the senses and of the vital energy in the yogic fire of self-control kindled by knowledge.

That is to say, they lose themselves in the contemplation of the Supreme.

28. Some sacrifice with material gifts; with austerities; with yoga; some with the acquiring and some with the imparting of knowledge. All these are sacrifices of stern vows and serious endeavour.

29. Others absorbed in the practices of the control of the vital energy sacrifice the outward in the inward and the inward in the outward, or check the flow of both the inward and the outward vital airs.

The reference here is to the three kinds of practices of the control of vital energy—puraka, rechaka, and kumbhaka.

30. Yet others, abstemious in food, sacrifice one form of vital energy

in another. All these know what sacrifice is and purge themselves of all impurities by sacrifice.

31. Those who partake of the residue of sacrifice—called amrita (ambrosia)—attain to everlasting Brahman. Even this world is not for a non-sacrificer; how then the next, O Kurusattama?

32. Even so various sacrifices have been described in the Vedas; know them all to proceed from action; knowing this thou shalt be released.

Action here means mental, physical and spiritual action. No sacrifice is possible without this triple action and no salvation without sacrifice. To know this and to put the knowledge into practice is to know the secret of sacrifice. In fine, unless man uses all his physical, mental and spiritual gifts in the service of mankind, he is a thief unfit for Freedom. He who uses his intellect only and spares his body is not a full sacrificer. Unless the mind and the body and the soul are made to work in unison, they cannot be adequately used for the service of mankind. Physical, mental and spiritual purity is essential for the harmonious working. Therefore man should concentrate on developing, purifying, and turning to the best of all his faculties.

33. Knowledge-sacrifice is better, O-Parantapa, than material sacrifice, for all action which does not bind finds its consummation in Knowledge (jnana).

Who does not know that works of charity performed without knowledge often result in great harm? Unless every act, however nobel its motive, is informed with knowledge, it lacks perfection. Hence the complete fulfillment of all action is in knowledge.

34. The masters of knowledge who have seen the Truth will impart to thee this Knowledge; learn it through humble homage and service and by repeated questioning.

The three conditions of knowledge—homage, repeated questioning and service—deserve to be carefully borne in mind in this age. Homage or obeisance means humility and service is a necessary accompaniment; else it would be mock homage. Repeated questioning is equally essential, for without a keen spirit of inquiry, there is no knowledge. All this presupposes devotion to and faith in the person approached. There can be no humility, much less service, without faith.

35. When thou hast gained this knowledge, O Pandava, thou shalt not again fall into such error; by virtue of it thou shalt see all beings without exception in thyself and thus in Me.

The adage 'Yatha pinde tatha brahmande'—'as with the self so with the universe') means the same thing. He who has attained Self-realization sees no difference between himself and others.

36. Even though thou be the most sinful of sinners, thou shalt cross the ocean of sin by the boat of knowledge.

37. As a blazing fire turns its fuel to ashes, O Arjuna, even so the fire of Knowledge turns all actions to ashes.

38. There is nothing in this world so purifying as Knowledge. He who is perfected by yoga finds it in himself in the fullness of time.

39. It is the man of faith who gains knowledge—the man who is intent on it and who has mastery over his senses; having gained knowledge, he comes ere long to the supreme peace.

40. But the man of doubt, without knowledge and without faith, is lost; for him who is given to doubt there is neither this world nor that beyond, nor happiness.

41. He who has renounced all action by means of yoga, who has severed all doubt by means of knowledge—him self-possessed, no actions bind, O Dhananjaya!

42. Therefore, with the sword of Self-realization sever thou this

doubt, bred of ignorance, which has crept into thy heart! Betake thyself to yoga and arise, O Bharata!

Thus ends the fourth discourse, entitled 'Jnana-Karma-Sannyasa-Yoga' in the converse of Lord Krishna and Arjuna, on the science of Yoga, as part of the knowledge of Brahman in the Upanishad called the Bhagawadgita.

DISCOURCE 5.

This discourse is devoted to showing that renunciation of action as such is impossible without the discipline of selfless action and that both are ultimately one.

Arjuna Said:

1. Thou laudest renunciation of actions, O Krishna, whilst at the same time thou laudest performance of action; tell me for a certainty which is the better.

The Lord Said:

2. Renunciation and performance of action both lead to salvation; but of the two, karmayoga (performance) is better than sannyasa (renunciation).

3. Him one should know as ever renouncing who has no dislikes and likes; for he who is free from the pairs of opposites is easily released from bondage.

That is, not renunciation of action but of attachment to the pairs determines true renunciation. A man who is always in action may be a good sannyasa (renouncer) and another who may be doing no work may well be a hypocrite. See III. 6.

4. It is the ignorant who speak of sankhya and yoga as different, not so those who have knowledge. He who is rightly established even in

one wins to the fruit of both.

The yogi engrossed in sankhya (knowledge)lives even in thought for the good of the world and attains the fruit of karmayoga by the sheer power of his thought. The karmayogi ever engrossed in unattached action naturally enjoys the peace of the jnanayogi.

5. The goal that the sankhyas attain is also reached by the yogins. He sees truly who sees both sankhya and yoga as one.

6. But renunciation, O Mahabahu, is hard to attain except by yoga; the ascetic equipped with yoga attains Brahman ere long.

7. The yogi who has cleared himself, has gained mastery over his mind and all his senses, who has become one with the Atman in all creation, although he acts he remains unaffected.

8. The yogi who has seen the Truth knows that it is not he that acts whilst seeing, hearing, touching, smelling, eating, walking, sleeping, or breathing,

9. Talking, letting go, holding fast, opening or closing the eyes—in the conviction that is the senses that are moving in their respective spheres.

So long as 'self' endures, this detachment cannot be achieved. A sensual man therefore may not shelter himself under the pretence that it is not he but his senses that are acting. Such a mischievous interpretation betrays a gross ignorance of the Gita and right conduct. The next shloka makes this clear.

10. He who dedicates his actions to Brahman and performs them without attachment is not smeared by sin, as the lotus-leaf by water.

11. Only with the body, mind and intellect and also with the senses, do the yogins perform action without attachment for the sake of self-purification.

12. A man of yoga obtains everlasting peace by abandoning the

fruit of action; the man ignorant of yoga, selfishly attached to fruit, remains bound.

13. Renouncing with the mind all actions, the dweller in the body, who is master of himself, rests happily in his city of nine gates, neither doing nor getting anything done.

The principal gates of the body are the two eyes, the two nostrils, the two ears, the mouth, and the two organs of excretion—though really speaking the countless pores of the skin are no less gates. If the gatekeeper always remains on the alert and performs his task, letting in or out only the objects that deserve ingress or egress, then of him it can truly be said that he has no part in the ingress or egress, but that he is a passive witness. He thus does nothing nor gets any thing done.

14. The Lord creates neither agency nor action for the world; neither does he connect action with its fruit. It is nature that is at work.

God is no doer. The inexorable law of karma prevails, and in the very fulfillment of the law—giving everyone his deserts, making everyone reap what he sows—lies God's abounding mercy and justice. In undiluted justice is mercy. Mercy which is inconsistent with justice is not mercy but its opposite. But man is not a judge knowing past, present, and future. So for him the law is reversed and mercy or forgiveness is the purest justice. Being himself ever liable to be judged he must accord to others what he would accord to himself, viz. forgiveness. Only by cultivating the spirit of forgiveness can he reach the state of a yogi, whom no actions bind, the man of even-mindedness, the man skilled in action.

15. The Lord does not take upon Himself anyone's vice or virtue; it is ignorance that veils knowledge and deludes all creatures.

The delusion lies in man arrogating to himself the authorship of action and the attributing to God the consequences thereof—punishment or reward as the case may be.

16. But to them whose ignorance is destroyed by the knowledge of Atman, this their knowledge, like the sun, reveals the Supreme.

17. Those whose intellect is suffused with That, whose self has become one with That, who abide in That, and whose end and aim is that, wipe out their sins with knowledge, and go whence there is no return.

18. The men of Self-realization look with an equal eye on a brahmana possessed of learning and humility, a cow, an elephant, a dog and even a dog-eater.

That is to say, they serve every one of them alike, according to the needs of each. Treating a brahmana and shwapaka (dog-eater) alike means that the wise man will suck the poison off a snake-bitten shwapaka with as much eagerness and readiness as he would from a snake-bitten brahmana.

19. In this very body they have conquered the round of birth and death, whose mind is anchored in sameness; for perfect Brahman is same to all, therefore in Brahman they rest.

As a man thinks, so he becomes, and therefore those whose minds are bent on being the same to all achieve that sameness and become one with Brahman.

20. He whose understanding is secure, who is undeluded, who knows Brahman and who rests in Brahman, will neither be glad to get what is pleasant, nor sad to get what is unpleasant.

21. He who has detached himself from contacts without, finds bliss in Atman; having achieved union with Brahman he enjoys eternal bliss.

He who has weaned himself from outward objects to the inner Atman is fitted for union with Brahman and the highest bliss. To withdraw oneself from contacts without and to bask in the sunshine of union with Brahman are two aspects of the same state, two sides of the same coin.

22. For the joys derived from sense-contacts are nothing but mines of misery; they have beginning and end, O Kaunteya; the wise man does not revel therein.

23. The man who is able even here on earth, ere he is released from the body, to hold out against the floodtide of lust and wrath,—he is a yogi, he is happy.

As a corpse has no likes and dislikes, no sensibility to pleasure and pain, even so he who though alive is dead to these, he truly lives, he is truly happy.

24. He who finds happiness only within, rest only within, light only within,—that yogi, having become one with nature, attains to oneness with Brahman.

25. They win oneness with Brahman—the seers whose sins are wiped out, whose doubts are resolved, who have mastered themselves, and who are engrossed in the welfare of all beings.

26. Rid of lust and wrath, masters of themselves, the ascetics who have realized Atman find oneness with Brahman everywhere around them.

27-28. That ascetic is ever free—who, having shut out the outward sense-contacts, sits with his gaze fixed between the brows, outward and inward breathing in the nostrils made equal; his senses, mind, and reason held in check; rid of longing, fear and wrath; and intent on Freedom.

These shlokas refer to some of the yogic practices laid down in the Yoga-sutras. A word of caution is necessary regarding these practices. They serve for the yogin the same purpose as athletics and gymnastics do for the bhogin (who pursues worldly pleasures). His physical exercises help the latter to keep his senses of enjoyment in full vigour. The yogic practices help the yogin to keep his body in condition and his senses in subjection. Men versed in these practices are rare in these days, and few of them turn them to good account. He who has achieved the preliminary stage on the path to self-discipline, he who has a passion for Freedom, and who having rid himself of the pairs of opposites has conquered fear, would do well to go in for these practices which will surely help him. It is such a disciplined man alone who can, through these practices, render his body a holy temple of God. Purity both of the mind and body is a sine qua non, without which these processes are likely, in the first instance, to lead a man astray and then drive him deeper into the slough of delusion. That this has been the result in some cases many know from actual experience. That is why that prince of yogins, Patanjali gave the first place to yamas (cardinal vows) and niyamas (casual vows), and held as eligible for yogic practices only those who have gone through the preliminary discipline.

The five cardinal vows are: non-violence, truth, non-stealing, celibacy, non-possession. The five casual vows are: bodily purity, contentment, the study of the scriptures, austerity, and meditation of God.

29. Knowing Me as the Acceptor of sacrifice and austerity, the great Lord of all the worlds, the Friend of all creation, the yogi attains to peace.

This shloka may appear to be in conflict with shlokas 14 and 15 of this discourse and similar ones in other discourses. It is not really so. Almighty God is Doer and non-Doer, Enjoyer and non-Enjoyer both. He is indescribably, beyond the power of human speech. Man somehow strives to have a glimpse of Him and in so doing invests Him with diverse and even contradictory attributes.

Thus ends the fifth discourse, entitled 'Sannyasa Yoga' in the converse of Lord Krishna and Arjuna, on the science of Yoga, as part of the knowledge of Brahman, in the Upanishad called the Bhagawadgita.

DISCOURCE 6.

This discourse deals with some of the means for the accomplishment of Yoga or the discipline of the mind and its activities.

The Lord Said:

1. He who performs all obligatory action, without depending on the fruit thereof, is a sannyasin and a yogin—not the man who neglects the sacrificial fire nor he who neglects action.

Fire here may be taken to mean all possible instruments of action. Fire was needed when sacrifices used to be performed with its help. Assuming that spinning were a means of universal service in this age, a man by neglecting the spinning wheel would not become a sannyasi.

2. What is called sannyasa, know thou to be yoga, O Pandava; for none can become a yogin who has not renounced selfish purpose.

3. For the man who seeks to scale the heights of yoga, action is said to be the means; for the same man, when he has scaled those heights, repose is said to be the means.

He who has purged himself of all impurities and who has achieved even-mindedness will easily achieve Self-realization. But this does not mean that he who has scaled the heights of yoga will disdain to work for the guidance of the world. On the contrary that work will be to him not only the breath of his nostrils, but also as natural to him as breathing. He will do so by the sheer force of will. See V. 4.

4. When a man is not attached either to the objects of sense or to actions and sheds all selfish purpose, then he is said to have scaled the heights of yoga.

5. By one's Self should one raise oneself, and not allow oneself to fall; for Atman (Self) alone is the friend of self, and Self alone is self's foe.

6. His Self alone is friend, who has conquered himself by his Self: but to him who has not conquered himself and is thus inimical to himself, even his Self behaves as foe.

7. Of him who has conquered himself and who rests in perfect calm the self is completely composed, in cold and heat, in pleasure and pain, in honour and dishonour.

8. The yogin who is filled with the contentment of wisdom and discriminative knowledge, who is firm as a rock, who has mastered his senses, and to whom a clod of earth, a stone and gold are the same, is possessed of yoga.

9. He excels who regards alike the boon companion, the friend, the enemy, the stranger, the mediator, the alien and the ally, as also the saint and the sinner.

10. Let the yogi constantly apply his thought to Atman remaining alone in a scheduled place, his mind and body in control, rid of desires and possessions.

11. Fixing for himself, in a pure spot, a firm seat, neither too high nor yet too low, covered with kusha grass, thereon a deerskin, and thereon a cloth;

12. Sitting on that seat, with mind concentrated, the functions of thought and sense of control, he should set himself to the practice of yoga for the sake of self-purification.

13. Keeping himself steady, holding the trunk, the neck and the head in a straight line and motionless, fixing his eye on the tip of his nose, and looking not around.

14. Tranquil in spirit, free from fear, steadfast in the vow of brahmacharya, holding his mind in control, the yogi should sit, with all his thoughts on Me, absorbed in Me.

Brahmacharya (usually translated 'celibacy') means not only sexual continence but observance of all the cardinal vows for the attainment of Brahman.

15. The yogi, who ever thus, with mind controlled, unites himself to Atman, wins the peace which culminates in Nirvana, the peace that is in Me.

16. Yoga is not for him who eats too much, nor for him who fasts too much, neither for him who sleeps too much, nor yet for him who is too wakeful.

17. To him who is disciplined in food and recreation, in effort in all activities, and in sleep and waking, yoga (discipline) becomes a relief from all ills.

18. When one's thought, completely controlled, rests steadily on only Atman, when one is free from longing for all objects of desire, then one is called a yogin.

19. As a taper in a windless spot flickers not, even so is a yogin, with his thought controlled, seeking to unite himself with Atman.

20. Where thought curbed by the practice of yoga completely ceases, where a man sits content within himself, Atman having seen Atman;

21. Where he experiences that endless bliss beyond the senses which can be grasped by reason alone; wherein established he swerves not from the Truth;

22. Where he holds no other gain greater than that which he has gained; and where, securely seated, he is not shaken by any calamity however great;

23. That state should be known as yoga (union with the Supreme), the disunion from all union with pain. This yoga must one practice with firm resolve and unwearying zeal.

24. Shaking oneself completely free from longings born of selfish purpose; reining in the whole host of senses, from all sides, with the mind itself;

25. With reason held securely by the will, he should gradually attain calm and with the mind established in Atman think of nothing.

26. Wherever the fickle and unsteady mind wanders, thence should it be reined and brought under the sole sway of Atman.

28. The yogin, cleansed of all stain, unites himself ever thus to Atman, easily enjoys the endless bliss of contact with Brahman.

29. The man equipped with yoga looks on all with an impartial eye, seeing Atman in all beings and all beings in Atman.

30. He who sees Me everywhere and everything in Me, never vanishes from Me nor I from him.

31. The yogin who, anchored in unity, worships Me abiding in all beings, lives and moves in me, no matter how he live and move.

So long as 'self' subsists, the Supreme Self is absent; when 'self' is extinguished, the Supreme Self is seen everywhere. Also see note on XIII. 23.

32. He who, by likening himself with others, senses pleasure and pain equally for all as for himself, is deemed to be the highest yogi, O Arjuna.

Arjuna Said:

33. I do not see, O Madhusudana, how this yoga, based on the equal-mindedness that Thou hast expounded to me, can steadily endure, because of fickleness (of the mind).

34. For fickle is the mind, O Krishna, unruly, overpowering and stubborn; to curb it is, I think, as hard as to curb the wind.

The Lord Said:

35. Undoubtedly, O Mahabahu, the mind is fickle and hard to curb; yet, O Kaunteya, it can be held in check by constant practice and dispassion.

36. Without self-restraint, yoga, I hold, is difficult to attain; but the self-governed soul can attain it by proper means, if he strives for it.

Arjuna Said:

37. If one, possessed of faith, but slack of effort, because of his mind straying from yoga, reach not perfection in yoga, what end does he come to, O Krishna?

38. Without a foothold, and floundering in the path to Brahman fallen from both, is he indeed not lost, O Mahabahu, like a dissipated cloud?

39. This my doubt, O Krishna, do thou dispel utterly; for there is to be found none other than thou to banish this doubt.

The Lord Said:

40. Neither in this world, nor in the next, can there be ruin for him, O Partha; no well-doer, oh loved one, meets with a sad end.

41. Fallen from yoga, a man attains the worlds of righteous souls, and having dwelt there for numberless years is then born in a house of pure and gentle blood.

42. Or he may even be born into a family of yogins, though such

birth as this is all too rare in this world.

43. There, O Kurunandana, he discovers the intellectual stage he had reached in previous birth, and thence he stretches forward again towards perfection.

44. By virtue of that previous practice he is borne on, whether he will it or not, even he with a desire to know yoga passes beyond the Vedic ritual.

45. But the yogi who perseveres in his striving, cleansed of sin, perfected through many births, reaches the highest state.

46. The yogin is deemed higher than the man of austerities; he is deemed also higher than the man of knowledge; higher is he than the man engrossed in ritual; therefore be thou a yogin, O Arjuna!

47. And among all yogins, he who worships Me with faith, his inmost self all rapt in Me, is deemed by me to be the best yogin.

Thus ends the sixth discourse entitled 'Dhyana Yoga' in the converse of Lord Krishna and Arjuna, on the science of Yoga, as part of the knowledge of Brahman in the Upanishad called the Bhagawadgita.

DISCOURCE 7.

With this discourse begins an exposition of the nature of Reality and the secret of devotion.

The Lord Said:

1. Hear, O Partha, how, with thy mind rivetted on me, by practicing yoga and making me the sole refuge, thou shalt, without doubt, know me fully.

2. I will declare to thee, in its entirety, this knowledge, combined with discriminative knowledge, which when thou hast known there remains here nothing more to be known.

3. Among thousands of men hardly one strives after perfection; among those who strive hardly one knows Me in truth.

4. Earth, Water, Fire, Air, Ether, Mind, Reason and Ego—thus eightfold is my prakriti divided.

The eightfold prakriti is substantially the same as the field described in XIII. 5 and the perishable Being in XV. 16.

5. This is My lower aspect; but know thou My other aspect, the higher— which is Jiva (the Vital Essence) by which, O Mahabahu, this world is sustained.

6. Know that these two compose the source from which all beings

spring; I am the origin and end of the entire universe.

7. There is nothing higher than I, O Dhananjaya; all this is strung on Me as a row of gems upon a thread.

8. In water I am the savour, O Kaunteya; in the sun and the moon I am the light; the syllable AUM in all the Vedas; the sound in ether, and manliness in men.

9. I am the sweet fragrance in earth; the brilliance in fire; the life in all beings; and the austerity in ascetics.

10. Know Me, O Partha, to be the primeval seed of all beings; I am the reason of rational beings and the splendour of the splendid.

11. Of the strong, I am the strength, divorced from lust and passion; in beings I am desire undivorced from righteousness.

12. Know that all the manifestations of the three gunas, sattva, rajas, and tamas, proceed from none but Me; yet I am not in them; they are in Me.

God is not dependent on them, they are dependent on Him. Without Him those various manifestations would be impossible.

13. Befogged by these manifestations of the three gunas, the entire world fails to recognize Me, the imperishable, as transcending them.

14. For this My divine delusive mystery made up of the three gunas is hard to pierce; but those who make Me their sole refuge pierce the veil.

15. The deluded evil-doers, lowest of men, do not see refuge in Me; for, by reason of this delusive mystery, they are bereft of knowledge and given to devilish ways.

16. Four types of well-doers are devoted to Me, O Arjuna; they are, O Bharatarshabha, the afflicted, the spiritual seeker, the material seeker, and the enlightened.

17. Of these the enlightened, ever attached to Me in single-minded devotion, is the best; for to the enlightened I am exceedingly dear and he is dear to Me.

18. All these are estimable indeed, but the enlightened I hold to be My very self; for he, the true yogi, is stayed on Me alone, the supreme goal.

19. At the end of many births the enlightened man finds refuge in Me; rare indeed is this great soul to whom 'Vasudeva is all'.

20. Men, bereft of knowledge by reason of various longings, seek refuge in other gods, pinning their faith on diverse rites, guided by their own nature.

21. Whatever form one desires to worship in faith and devotion, in that very form I make that faith of his secure.

22. Possessed of that faith he seeks a propitiate that one, and obtains therethrough his longings, dispensed in truth by none but Me.

23. But limited is the fruit that falls to those shortsighted ones; those who worship the gods go to the gods, those who worship Me come unto Me.

24. Not knowing My transcendent, imperishable, supreme character, the undiscerning think Me who am unmanifest to have become manifest.

25. Veiled by the delusive mystery created by My unique power, I am not manifest to all; this bewildered world does not recognize Me, birthless and changeless.

Having the power to create this world of sense and yet unaffected by it, He is described as having unique power.

26. I know, O Arjuna, all creatures past, present and to be; but no one knows Me.

27. All creatures in this universe are bewildered, O Parantapa, by virtue of the delusion of the pairs of opposite sprung from likes and dislikes, O Bharata.

28. But those virtuous men whose sin has come to an end, freed from delusion and of the pairs of opposites, worship Me in steadfast faith.

29. Those who endeavour for freedom from age and death by taking refuge in Me, know in full that Brahman, Adhyatma and all Karma.

30. Those who know Me, including **Adhibhuta, Adhidaiva, Adhiyajna,** possessed of even-mindedness, they know Me even at the time of passing away.

The terms in italics are defined in the next discourse the subject of which is indicated in 29-30. The sense is that every nook and cranny of the universe is filled with Brahman, that He is the sole Agent of all action, and that the man who imbued to Him, becomes one with Him at the time of passing hence. All his desires are extinguished in his vision of Him and he wins his freedom.

Thus ends the seventh discourse, entitled 'Jananvijnana Yoga' in the converse of Lord Krishna and Arjuna, on the science of Yoga, as part of the knowledge of Brahman in the Upanishad called the Bhagawadgita.

DISCOURCE 8.

The nature of the Supreme is further expounded in this discourse.

Arjuna Said:

1. What is that Brahman? What is Adhyatma? What Karma, O Purushottama? What is called Adhibhuta? And what Adhidaiva?

2. And who here in this body is Adhiyajna and how? And how at the time of death art Thou to be known by the self-controlled?

The Lord Said:

3. The Supreme, the Imperishable is Brahman; its manifestation is Adhyatma; the creative process whereby all beings are created is called Karma.

4. Adhibhuta is My perishable form; Adhidaivata is the individual self in that form; and O best among the embodied, Adhiyajna am I in this body, purified by sacrifice.

That is, from Imperishable Unmanifest down to the perishable atom everything in the universe is the Supreme and an expression of the Supreme. Why then should mortal man arrogate to himself authorship of anything rather than do His bidding and dedicate all action to Him?

5. And he who, at the last hour remembering Me only, departs

leaving the body, enters into Me; of that there is no doubt.

6. Or whatever form a man continually contemplates, that same he remembers in the hour of death, and to that very form he goes, O Kaunteya.

7. Therefore at all times remember Me and fight on; thy mind and reason thus on Me fixed thou shalt surely come to Me.

8. With thought steadied by constant practice, and wandering nowhere, he who meditates on the Supreme Celestial Being, O Partha, goes to Him.

9-10. Whoso, at the time of death, with unwavering mind, with devotion, and fixing the breath rightly between the brows by the power of yoga, meditates on the Sage, the Ancient, the Ruler, subtler than the subtlest, the Supporter of all, the Inconceivable, glorious as the sun beyond the darkness,—he goes to that Supreme Celestial Being.

11. That which the knowers of the Vedas call the Imperishable (or that word which the knowers of the Vedas repeat), wherein the ascetics freed from passion enter and desiring which they practice brahmacharya, that Goal (or Word) I will declare to thee in brief.

12. Closing all the gates, locking up the mind in the hridaya, fixing his breath within the head, rapt in yogic meditation;

13. Whoso departs leaving the body uttering AUM—Brahman in one syllable—repeatedly thinking on Me, he reaches the highest state.

14. That yogi easily wins to Me, O Partha, who, ever attached to Me, constantly remembers Me with undivided mind.

15. Great souls, having come to Me, reach the highest perfection; they come not again to birth, unlasting and (withal) an abode of misery.

16. From the world of Brahma down, all the worlds are subject to

return, O Arjuna; but on coming to Me there is no rebirth.

17. Those men indeed know what is Day and what is Night, who know that Brahma's day lasts a thousand yugas and that his night too is a thousand yugas long.

That is to say, our day and night of a dozen hours each are less than the infinitesimal fraction of a moment in that vast cycle of time. Pleasures pursued during these incalculably small moments are as illusory as a mirage. Rather than waste these brief moments, we should devote them to serving God through service of mankind. On the other hand, our time is such a small drop in the ocean of eternity that if we fail of our object here, viz. Self-realization, we need not despair. She should bide our time.

18. At the coming of Day all the manifest spring forth from the Unmanifest, and at the coming of Night they are dissolved into that same Unmanifest.

Knowing this too, man should understand that he has very little power over things, the round of birth and death is ceaseless.

19. This same multitude of creatures come to birth, O Partha, again and again; they are dissolved at the coming of Night, whether they will or not; and at the break of Day they are re-born.

20. But higher than the Unmanifest is another Unmanifest Being, everlasting, which perisheth not when all creatures perish.

21. This Unmanifest, named the Imperishable, is declared to be the highest goal. For those who reach it there is no return. That is my highest abode.

22. This Supreme Being, O Partha, may be won by undivided devotion; in It all beings dwell, by It all is pervaded.

23. Now I will tell thee, Bharatarshabha, the conditions which determine the exemption from return, as also the return, of yogins

after they pass away hence.

24. Fire, Light, Day, the Bright Fortnight, the six months of the Northern Solstice—through these departing men knowing Brahman go to Brahman.

25. Smoke, Night, the Dark Fortnight, the six months of the Southern Solstice—Therethrough the yogin attains to the lunar light and thence returns.

I do not understand the meaning of these two shlokas. They do not seem to me to be consistent with the teaching of the Gita. The Gita teaches that he whose heart is meek with devotion, who is devoted to unattached action and has seen the Truth must win salvation, no matter when he dies. These shlokas seem to run counter to this. They may perhaps be stretched to mean broadly that a man of sacrifice, a man of light, a man who has known Brahman finds release from birth if he retains that enlightenment at the time of death, and that on the contrary the man who has none of these attributes goes to the world of the moon—not at all lasting—and returns to birth. The moon, after all, shines with borrowed light.

26. These two paths—bright and dark—are deemed to be the eternal paths of the world; by the one a man goes to return not, by the other he returns again.

The Bright one may be taken to mean the path of knowledge and the dark one that of ignorance.

27. The Yogin knowing these two paths falls not into delusion, O Partha; therefore, at all times, O Arjuna, remain steadfast in yoga.

"Will not fall into delusion" means that he who knows the two paths and has known the secret of even-mindedness will not take the path of ignorance.

28. Whatever fruit of good deeds is laid down as accruing from (a study of) the Vedas, from sacrifices, austerities, and acts of charity—

all that the yogin transcends, on knowing this, and reaches the Supreme and Primal Abode.

He who has achieved even-mindedness by dint of devotion, knowledge and service not only obtains the fruit of all his good actions, but also wins salvation.

Thus ends the eighth discourse entitled 'Brahma Yoga' in the converse of Lord Krishna and Arjuna, on the science of Yoga, as part of the knowledge of Brahman in the Upanishad called the Bhagawadgita.

DISCOURCE 9.

This discourse reveals the glory of devotion.

The Lord Said:

1. I will now declare to thee, who art uncensorious, this mysterious knowledge, together with discriminative knowledge, knowing which thou shalt be released from ill.

2. This is the king of sciences, the king of mysteries, pure and sovereign, capable of direct comprehension, the essence of dharma, easy to practice, changeless.

3. Men who have no faith in this doctrine, O Parantapa, far from coming to Me, return repeatedly to the path of this world of death.

4. By Me, unmanifest in form, this whole world is pervaded; all beings are in Me, I am not in them.

5. And yet those beings are not in Me. That indeed is My unique power as Lord! Sustainer of all beings, I am not in them; My Self brings them into existence.

The sovereign power of God lies in this mystery, this miracle, that all beings are in Him and yet not in Him, He in them and yet not in them. This is the description of God in the language of mortal man. Indeed He soothes man by revealing to him all His aspects by using all kinds of paradoxes. All beings are in him inasmuch as all creation is His; but as He transcends it all, as He really is not the author of it all, it may be said with equal truth that the beings are not in Him. He really is in all His true devotees, He is not, according to them, in those who deny Him. What is this if not a mystery, a miracle of God?

6. As the mighty wind, moving everywhere, is ever contained in ether, even so know that all beings are contained in Me.

7. All beings, O Kaunteya, merge into my prakriti, at the end of a kalpa, and I send them forth again when a kalpa begins.

8. Resorting to my prakriti, I send forth again and again this multitude of beings, powerless under the sway of prakriti.

9. But all this activity, O Dhananjaya, does not bind Me, seated as one indifferent, unattached to it.

10. With me as Presiding Witness, prakriti gives birth to all that moves and does not move; and because of this, O Kaunteya, the wheel of the world keeps going.

11. Not knowing My transcendent nature as the sovereign Lord of all beings, fools condemn Me incarnated as man.

For they deny the existence of God and do not recognize the Director in the human body.

12. Vain are the hopes, actions and knowledge of those witless ones who have resorted to the delusive nature of monsters and devils.

13. But those great souls who resort to the divine nature, O Partha, know Me as the Imperishable Source of all beings and worship Me with an undivided mind.

14. Always declaring My glory, striving in steadfast faith, they do Me devout homage; ever attached to Me, they worship Me.

15. Yet others, with knowledge-sacrifice, worship Me, who am to be seen everywhere, as one, as different or as many.

16. I am the sacrificial vow; I am the sacrifice; I the ancestral oblation; I the herb; I the sacred text; I the clarified butter; I the fire; I the burnt offering.

17. Of this universe I am the Father, Mother, Creator, Grandsire: I am what is to be known, the sacred syllable AUM; the rig, the Saman and the Yajus;

18. I am the Goal, the Sustainer, the Lord, the Witness, the Abode, the Refuge, the Friend; the Origin, the End the Preservation, the Treasurehouse, the Imperishable Seed.

19. I give heat; I hold back and pour forth rain; I am deathlessness and also death. O Arjuna, Being and not-Being as well.

20. Followers of the three Vedas, who drink the soma juice and are purged of sin, worship Me with sacrifice and pray for going to heaven; they reach the holy world of the gods and enjoy in heaven the divine joys of the gods.

The reference is to the sacrificial ceremonies and rites in vogue in the days of the Gita. We cannot definitely say what they were like nor what the soma juice exactly was.

21. They enjoy the vast world of heaven, and their merit spent, they enter the world of the mortals; thus those who, following the Vedic law, long for the fruit of their action earn but the round of birth and death.

22. As for those who worship Me, thinking on Me alone and nothing else, ever attached to Me, I bear the burden of getting them what they need.

There are thus three unmistakable marks of a true yogi or bhakta—even-mindedness, skill in action, undivided devotion. These three must be completely harmonized in a yogi. Without devotion there is no even-mindedness, without even-mindedness no devotion, and without skill in action devotion and even-minded might well be a pretense.

23. Even those who, devoted to other gods, worship them in full faith, even they, O Kaunteya, worship none but Me, though not according to the rule.

'Not according to the rule' means not knowing Me as the Impersonal and the Absolute.

24. For I am the Acceptor and the Director of all sacrifices; but not recognizing Me as I am, they go astray.

25. Those who worship the gods go to the gods; those who worship the manes go to the manes; those who worship the spirits go to the spirits; but those who worship Me come to Me.

26. Any offering of leaf, flower, fruit or water, made to Me in devotion, by an earnest soul, I lovingly accept.

That is to say, it is the Lord in every being whom we serve with devotion who accepts the service.

27. Whatever thou doest, whatever thou eatest, whatever thou offerest as sacrifice or gift, whatever austerity thou dost perform, O kaunteya, dedicate all to Me.

28. So doing thou shalt be released from the bondage of action, yielding good and evil fruit; having accomplished both renunciation and performance, thou shalt be released (from birth and death) and come unto Me.

29. I am the same to all beings; with Me there is non disfavoured, none favoured; but those who worship Me with devotion are in Me and I in them.

30. A sinner, howsoever great, if he turns to Me with undivided devotion, must indeed be counted a saint; for he has a settled resolve.

The undivided devotion subdues both his passions and his evil deeds.

31. For soon he becomes righteous and wins everlasting peace; know for a certainty, O kaunteya, that my bhakta never perishes.

32. For finding refuge in Me, even those who though are born of the womb of sin, women, vaishyas, and shudras too, reach the supreme goal.

33. How much more then, the pure brahmanas and seer-kings who are my devotees? Do thou worship Me, therefore, since thou hast come to this fleeting and joyless world.

34. On Me fix thy mind, to Me bring thy devotion, to Me offer thy sacrifice, to Me make thy obeisance; thus having attached thyself to Me and made Me thy end and aim, to Me indeed shalt thou come.

Thus ends the ninth discourse entitled 'Rajavidya-rajaguhya Yoga' in the converse of Lord Krishna and Arjuna, on the science of Yoga, as part of the knowledge of Brahman in the Upanishad called the Bhagawadgita.

DISCOURCE 10.

For the benefit of His devotees, the Lord gives in this discourse a glimpse of His divine manifestations.

The Lord Said:

1. Yet once more, O Mahabahu, here My supreme word, which I will utter to thee, gratified one, for thy benefit.

2. Neither the gods nor the great seers know My origin; for I am, every way, the origin of them both.

3. He who knows Me, the great lord of the worlds, as birthless and without beginning, he among mortals, undeluded, is released from sins.

4. Discernment, knowledge, freedom from delusion, long suffering, truth, self-restraint, inward calm, pleasure, pain, birth, death, fear and fearlessness;

5. Non-violence, even-mindedness, contentment, austerity, beneficence, good and ill fame,—all these various attributes of creatures proceed verily from Me.

6. The seven great seers, the ancient four, and the Manus too were born of Me and of My mind, and of them were born all the creatures in the world.

7. He who knows in truth My immanence and My yoga becomes gifted with unshakable yoga; of this there is no doubt.

8. I am the source of all, all proceeds from me; knowing this, the wise worship Me with hearts full of devotion.

9. With me in their thoughts, their whole soul devoted to Me, teaching one another, with me ever on their lips, they live in contentment and joy.

10. To these, ever in tune with Me worshipping me with affectionate devotion, I give the power of selfless action, whereby they come to Me.

11. Out of every compassion for them, I who dwell in their hearts, destroy the darkness, born of ignorance, with the refulgent lamp of knowledge.

Arjuna Said:

12. Lord! Thou art the supreme Brahman, the supreme Abode, the supreme Purifier! Everlasting Celestial Being, the Primal God, Unborn, All-pervading.

13. Thus have all the seers—the divine seer Narada, Asita, Devala, Vyasa—declared Thee; and Thou Thyself dost tell me so.

14. All that Thou tellest me is true, I know, O Keshava, verily, Lord, neither the gods nor the demons know Thy manifestation.

15. Thyself alone Thou knowest by Thyself, O Purushottama, O Source and Lord of all beings, God of Gods, O Ruler of the universe.

16. Indeed Thou oughtest to tell me of all Thy manifestations, without a remainder, whereby Thou dost pervade the worlds.

17. O Yogin! constantly meditating on Thee, how am I to know Thee? In what various aspects am I to think of Thee, O Lord?

18. Recount to me yet again, in full detail, Thy unique power and Thy immanence, O Janardana! For my ears cannot be sated with listening to Thy life-giving words.

The Lord Said:

19. Yea, I will unfold to thee, O Kurushreshtha, My divine manifestations,—the chiefest only; for there is no limit to their extent.

20. I am the Atman, O Gudakesha, seated in the heart of every being; I am the beginning, the middle and the end of all beings.

21. Of the Adityas I am Vishnu; of luminaries, the radiant Sun; of Maruts, I am Marichi; of constellations, the moon.

22. Of the Vedas I am the Sama Veda; of the gods Indra; of the senses I am the mind; of beings I am the consciousness.

23. Of Rudras I am Shankara; of Yakshas and Rakshasas Kubera; of Vasus I am the Fire; of mountains Meru.

24. Of priests, O Partha, know Me to be the chief Brihaspati; of army captains I am Kartikeya; and of waters the ocean.

25. Of the great seers I am Bhrigu; of words I am the one syllable 'AUM'; of sacrifices I am the Japa sacrifice; of things immovable, the Himalaya.

26. Of all trees I am Ashvattha; of the divine seers, Narada; of the heavenly choir I am Chitraratha; of the perfected I am Kapila the ascetic.

27. Of horses, Know Me to be the Uchchaihshravas born with Amrita; of mighty elephants I am Airavata; of men, the monarch.

28. Of weapons, I am Vajra; of cows, Kamadhenu; I am Kandarpa, the god of generation; of serpants I am Vasuki.

29. Of cobras I am Anata; of water-dwellers I am Varuna; of the manes I am Aryaman; and of the chastisers, Yama.

30. Of demons I am Prahlada; of reckoners, the time; of beasts I am the lion; and of birds, Garuda.

31. Of cleansing agents I am the Wind; of wielders of weapons, Rama; of fishes I am the crocodile; of rivers the Ganges.

32. Of creations I am the beginning, end and middle, O Arjuna; of sciences, the science of spiritual knowledge; of debators, the right argument.

33. Of letters, the letter A; of compounds I am the dvandva; I am the imperishable Time; I am the creator to be seen everywhere.

34. All-seizing Death am I, as the source of things to be; in feminine virtues I am Kirti (glory), Shri (beauty), Vak (speech), Smriti (memory), Medha (intelligence), Dhriti (constancy) and Kshama (forgiveness).

35. Of Saman hymns I am Brihat Saman; of metres, Gayatri; of months I am Margashirsha; of seasons, the spring.

36. Of deceivers I am the dice-play; of the splendid the splendour; I am victory, I am resolution, I am the goodness of the good.

The 'dice-play of deceivers' need not alarm one. For the good and evil nature of things in not the matter in question, it is the directing and immanent power of God that is being described. Let the deceivers also know that they are under God's rule and judgment and put away their pride and deceit.

37. Of Vrishnis I am Vasudeva; of Pandavas Dhananjaya; of ascetics I am Vyasa; and of seers, Ushanas.

38. I am the rod of those that punish; the strategy of those seeking victory; of secret things I am silence, and the knowledge of those that know.

39. Whatever is the seed of every being, O Arjuna, that am I; there is nothing, whether moving or fixed, that can be without Me.

40. there is no end to my divine manifestations; what extent of them I have told thee now is only by way of illustration.

41. Whatever is glorious, beautiful and mighty know thou that all such has issued from a fragment of My splendour.

42. But why needest thou to learn this at great length, O Arjuna? With but a part of Myself I stand upholding this universe.

Thus ends the tenth discourse, entitled 'Vibhuti Yoga' in the converse of Lord Krishna and Arjuna, on the science of Yoga, as part of the knowledge of Brahman, in the Upanishad called the Bhagawadgita.

DISCOURCE 11.

In this discourse the Lord reveals to Arjuna's vision what Arjuna has heard with his ears—the Universal Form of the Lord. This discourse is a favourite with the Bhaktas. Here there is no argument, there is pure poetry. Its solemn music* reverberates in one's ears and it is not possible to tire of reading it again and again.

*The music, of course, of the original! In translation, 'the glory is gone'. For a very free rendering which brings out some at least of the haunting music of the original the reader must go to Sir Edwin Arnold's flowing stanzas.

Arjuna Said:

1. Out of Thy grace towards me, thou hast told me the supreme mystery revealing the knowledge of the Supreme; it has banished my delusion.

2. Of the origin and destruction of beings I have heard from Thee in full detail, as also Thy imperishable ajesty [sic], O Kamala-patraksha!

3. Thou art indeed as Thou hast described Thyself, Parameshvara! I do crave to behold, now, that form of Thine as Ishvara.

4. If, Lord, thou thinkest it possible for me to bear the sight, reveal to me, O Yogeshvara, Thy imperishable form.

The Lord Said:

5. Behold, O Partha, my forms divine in their hundreds and thousands, infinitely diverse, infinitely various in color and aspect.

6. Behold the Adityas, the Vasus, the Rudras, the two Ashwins, the Maruts; behold, O Bharata, numerous marvels never revealed before.

7. Behold today, O Gudakesha, in my body, the whole universe, moving and unmoving, all in one, and whatever else thou cravest to see.

8. But thou canst not see Me with these thine own eyes. I give thee the eye divine; behold My sovereign power!

Sanjaya Said:

9. With these words, O King, the great Lord of Yoga, Hari, then revealed to Partha His supreme form as Ishvara.

10. With many mouths and many eyes, many wondrous aspects, many divine ornaments, and many brandished weapons divine.

11. Wearing divine garlands and vestments, annointed with divine perfumes, it was the form of God, all-marvellous [sic], infinite, seen everywhere.

12. Were the splendour of a thousand suns to shoot forth all at once in the sky that might perchance resemble the splendour of that Mighty One.

13. Then did Pandava see the whole universe in its manifold divisions gathered as one in the body of that God of gods.

14. Then Dhananjaya, wonderstruck and thrilled in every fibre of his being, bowed low his head before the Lord, addressing Him thus with folded hands.

Arjuna Said:

15. With Thy form, O Lord, I see all the gods and the diverse multitudes of beings, the Lord Brahma, on his lotus-throne and all the seers and serpents divine.

16. With many arms and bellies, mouths and eyes, I see Thy infinite form everywhere. Neither Thy end, nor middle, nor beginning, do I see, O Lord of the Universe, Universal-formed!

17. With crown and mace and disc, a mass of effulgence, gleaming everywhere I see Thee, so dazzling to the sight, bright with the splendour of the fiery sun blazing from all sides,—incomprehensible.

18. Thou art the Supreme Imperishable worthy to be known; Thou art the final resting place of this universe; Thou art the changeless guardian of the Eternal Dharma; Thou art, I believe, the Everlasting Being.

19. Thou hast no beginning, middle nor end; infinite is Thy might; arms innumerable; for eyes, the sun and the moon; Thy mouth a blazing fire, overpowering the universe with Thy radiance.

20. By Thee alone are filled the spaces between heaven and earth and all the quarters; at the sight of this Thy wondrous terrible form, the three worlds are sore oppressed, O Mahatman!

21. Here, too, the multitudes of gods are seen to enter Thee; some awe-struck praise Thee with folded arms; the hosts of great seers and siddhas, 'All Hail' on their lips, hymn Thee with songs of praise.

22. The Rudras, Adityas, Vasus, Sadhyas, all the gods, the twin Ashwins, Maruts, Manes, the hosts of Gandharvas, Yakshas, Asuras and Siddhas— all gaze on Thee in wonderment.

23. At the sight of thy mighty form, O Mahabahu, many-mouthed, with eyes, arms, thighs and feet innumerable, with many vast bellies, terrible with many jaws, the worlds feel fearfully oppressed, and so do I.

24. For as I behold Thee touching the sky, glowing, numerous-hued with gaping mouths and wide resplendent eyes, I feel oppressed in my innermost being; no peace nor quiet I find, O Vishnu!

25. As I see Thy mouths with fearful jaws, resembling the Fire of Doom, I lose all sense of direction, and find no relief. Be gracious, O Devesha, O Jagannivasa!

26. All the sons of Dhritarashtra, and with them the crowd of kings, Bhishma, Drona, and that Karna too, as also our chief warriors—

27. Are hastening into the fearful jaws of Thy terrible mouths. Some indeed, caught between Thy teeth, are seen, their heads being crushed to atoms.

28. As rivers, in their numerous torrents, run head-long to the sea, even so the heroes of the world of men rush into Thy flaming mouths.

29. As moths, fast-flying, plunge into blazing fire, straight to their doom, even so these rush headlong into Thy mouths, to their destruction.

30. Devouring all these from all sides, Thou lappest them with Thy flaming tongues; Thy fierce rays blaze forth, filling the whole universe with their lustre.

31. Tell me, Lord, who Thou art so dread of form! Hail to Thee, O Devavara! Be gracious! I desire to know Thee, Primal Lord; for I comprehend not what Thou dost.

The Lord Said:

32. Doom am I, full-ripe, dealing death to the worlds, engaged in devouring mankind. Even without slaying them not one of the warriors, ranged for battle against thee, shall survive.

33. Therefore, do thou arise, and win renown! Defeat thy foes and enjoy a thriving kingdom. By Me have these already been destroyed;

be thou no more than an instrument, O Savyasachin!

34. Drona, Bhishma, Jayadratha and Karna, as also the other warrior chiefs—already slain by Me—slay thou! Fight! Victory is thine over the foes in the field.

Sanjaya Said:

35. Hearing this world of Keshava, crown-wearer Arjuna folded his hands, and trembling made obeisance. Bowing and all hesitant, in faltering accents, he proceeded to address Krishna once more.

Arjuna Said:

36. Right proper it is, O Hrishikesha, that Thy praise should stir the world to gladness and tender emotion; the Rakshasas in fear fly to every quarter and all the hosts of Siddhas do reverent homage.

37. And why should they not bow down to Thee, O Mahatma? Thou art the First Creator, greater even than Brahma. O Ananta, O Devesha, O Jagannivasa, Thou art the Imperishable, Being, not-Being, and That which transcends even these.

38. Thou art the Primal God, the Ancient Being; Thou art the Final Resting Place of this Universe; Thou art the Knower, the 'to-be-known', the Supreme Abode; by Thee, O Myriad-formed, is the universe pervaded.

39. Thou art Vayu, Yama, Agni, Varuna, Shashanka, Prajapati, and Prapitamaha! All Hail to Thee, a thousand times all hail! Again and yet again all hail to Thee!

40. All hail to Thee from before and behind! all hail to Thee from every side, O All; Thy prowess is infinite, Thy might is measureless! Thou holdest all; therefore Thou art all.

41. If ever in carelessness, thinking of Thee as comrade, I addressed Thee saying, 'O Krishna!', 'O Yadava!' not knowing Thy greatness, in negligence or in affection,

42. If ever I have been rude to Thee in jest, whilst at play, at rest-time, or at meals, whilst alone or in company, O Achyuta, forgive Thou my fault—I beg of Thee, O Incomprehensible!

43. Thou art Father of this world, of the moving and the un-moving; thou art its adored, its worthiest, Master; there is none equal to Thee; how then any greater than Thee? Thy power is matchless in the three worlds.

44. Therefore, I prostrate myself before Thee, and beseech Thy grace, O Lord adorable! As father with son, as comrade with comrade, so shouldst Thou bear, beloved Lord, with me, Thy loved one.

45. I am filled with joy to see what never was seen before, and yet my heart is oppressed with fear. Show me that original form of Thine, O Lord! Be gracious, Devesha, O Jagannivasa!

46. I crave to see Thee even as Thou wast, with crown, with mace, and disc in hand; wear Thou, once more, that four-armed form, O thousand-armed Vishvamurti!

The Lord Said:

47. It is to favour thee, O Arjuna, that I have revealed to thee, by My own unique power, this My form Supreme, Resplendent, Universal, Infinite, Primal—which none save thee has ever seen.

48. Not by the study of the Vedas, not by sacrifice, not by the study of other scriptures, not by gifts, nor yet by performance of rites or of fierce austerities can I, in such a form, be seen by any one save thee in the world of men, O Kurupravira!

49. Be thou neither oppressed nor bewildered to look on this awful form of Mine. Banish thy fear, ease thy mind, and lo! behold Me once again as I was.

Sanjaya Said.

50. So said Vasudeva to Arjuna, and revealed to him once more His original form. Wearing again His form benign, the Mahatma consoled him terrified.

Arjuna Said.

51. Beholding again thy benign human form I am come to myself and once more in my normal state.

The Lord Said:

52. Very hard to behold is that form of Mine which thou hast seen; even the gods always yearn to see it.

53. Not by the Vedas, not by penance, nor by gifts, nor yet by sacrifice, can any behold Me in the form that thou hast seen.

54. But by single-minded devotion, O Arjuna, I may in this form be known and seen, and truly entered into, O Parantapa!

55. He alone comes to me, O Pandava, who does My work, who has made Me his goal, who is My devotee, who has renounced attachment, who has ill-will toward none.

Thus ends the eleventh discourse, entitled 'Vishvarupadarshana Yoga' in the converse of Lord Krishna and Arjuna, on the science of Yoga as part of the knowledge of Brahman in the Upanishad called the Bhagawadgita.

DISCOURCE 12.

Thus we see that vision of God is possible only through single-minded devotion. Contents of devotion must follow as a matter of course. This twelfth discourse should be learnt by hard even if all discourses are not. It is one of the shortest. The marks of a devotee should be carefully noted.

Arjuna Said:

1. Of the devotees who thus worship Thee, incessantly attached, and those who worship the Imperishable Unmanifest, which are the better yogins?

The Lord Said:

2. Those I regard as the best yogins who, riveting their minds Me, ever attached, worship Me, with the highest faith.

3. But those who worship the Imperishable, the indefinable, the Unmanifest, the Omnipresent, the Unthinkable, the Rock-seated, the Immovable, the Unchanging,

4. Keeping the whole host of senses in complete control, looking on all with an impartial eye, engrossed in the welfare of all beings—these come indeed to Me.

5. Greater is the travail of those whose mind is fixed on the Unmanifest; for it is hard for embodied mortals to gain the Unmanifest—Goal.

Mortal man can only imagine the Unmanifest, the Impersonal, and as his language fails him he often negatively describes It as 'Neti', 'Neti' (Not That, Not That). And so even iconoclasts are at bottom no better than idol-worshippers. To worship a book, to go to church, or to pray with one's face in a particular direction—all these are forms of worshipping the Formless in an image or idol. And yet, both the idol-breaker and the idol-worshipper cannot lose sight of the fact that there is something which is beyond all form, Unthinkable, Formless, Impersonal, Changeless. The highest goal of the devotee is to become one with the object of his devotion. The bhakta extinguishes himself and merges into, becomes, Bhagvan. This state can best be reached by devoting oneself to some form, and so it is said that the short cut to the Unmanifest is really the longest and the most difficult.

6. But those who casting all their actions on Me, making Me their all in all, worship Me with the meditation of undivided devotion,

7. Of such, whose thoughts are centered on Me, O Partha, I become ere long the Deliverer from the ocean of this world of death.

8. On Me set thy mind, on Me rest thy conviction; thus without doubt shalt thou remain only in Me hereafter.

9. If thou canst not set thy mind steadily on Me, then by the method of constant practice seek to win Me, O Dhananjaya.

10. If thou art also unequal to this method of constant practice, concentrate on service for Me; even thus serving Me thou shalt attain perfection.

11. If thou art unable even to do this, then dedicating all to Me, with mind controlled, abandon the fruit of action.

12. Better is knowledge than practice, better than knowledge is concentration, better than concentration is renunciation of the fruit of all action, from which directly issues peace.

'Practice' (abhyasa) is the practice of the yoga of meditation and control of psychic processes; 'knowledge' (jnana) is intellectual effort; 'concentration' (dhyana) is devoted worship. If as a result of all this there is no renunciation of the fruit of action, 'practice' is no 'practice', 'knowledge' is no 'knowledge', and 'concentration' is no 'concentration'.

13. Who has ill-will towards none, who is friendly and compassionate, who has shed all thought of 'mine' or 'I', who regards pain and pleasure alike, who is long-suffering;

14. Who is ever content, gifted with yoga, self-restrained, of firm conviction, who has dedicated his mind and reason to Me—that devotee (bhakta) of Mine is dear to Me.

15. Who gives no trouble to the world, to whom the world causes no trouble, who is free from exultation, resentment, fear and vexation,—that man is dear to Me.

16. Who expects naught, who is pure, resourceful, unconcerned, untroubled, who indulges in no undertakings,—that devotee of Mine is dear to Me.

17. Who rejoices not, neither frets nor grieves, who covets not, who abandons both good and ill—that devotee of Mine is dear to Me.

18. Who is same to foe and friend, who regards alike respect and disrespect, cold and heat, pleasure and pain, who is free from attachment;

19. Who weighs in equal scale blame and praise, who is silent, content with whatever his lot, who owns no home, who is of steady mind,—that devotee of Mine is dear to Me.

20. They who follow this essence of dharma, as I have told it, with faith, keeping Me as their goal,—those devotees are exceeding dear to Me.

Thus ends the twelfth discourse entitled 'Bhakti Yoga' in the converse of Lord Krishna and Arjuna, on the science of Yoga, as part of the knowledge of Brahman in the Upanishad called the Bhagawadgita.

DISCOURCE 13.

This discourse treats of the distinction between the body (not-Self) and the Atman (the Self).

The Lord Said:

1. This body, O Kaunteya, is called the Field; he who knows it is called the knower of the Field by those who know.

2. And understand Me to be, O Bharata, the knower of the Field in all the Fields; and the knowledge of the Field and the knower of the Field, I hold, is true knowledge.

3. What the Field is, what its nature, what its modifications, and whence is what, as also who He is, and what His power—hear this briefly from Me.

4. This subject has been sung by seers distinctively and in various ways, in different hymns as also in aphoristic texts about Brahman well reasoned and unequivocal.

5. The great elements, Individuation, Reason, the Unmanifest, the ten senses, and the one (mind), and the five spheres of the senses;

6. Desire, dislike, pleasure, pain, association, consciousness, cohesion— this, in sum, is what is called the Field with its modifications.

The great elements are Earth, Water, Fire, Air and Ether. 'Individuation' is the thought of I, or that the body is 'I'; the 'Unmanifest' is prakriti or maya; the ten senses are the five senses of perception—smell, taste, sight, touch and hearing, and the five organs of action, viz.: the hands, the feet, the tongue, and the two organs of excretion. The five spheres or objects of the senses are smell, savour, form, touch, and sound. 'Association' is the property of the different organs to co-operate. Dhriti is not patience or constancy but cohesion, i.e. the property of all the atoms in the body to hold together; from 'individuation' springs this cohesion.

Individuation is inherent in the unmanifest prakriti. The undeluded man is he who can cast off the individuation or ego, and having done so the shock of an inevitable thing like death and pairs of opposites caused by sense-contacts fail to affect him. The Field, subject to all its modifications, has to be abandoned in the end by the enlightened and the unenlightened alike.

7. Freedom from pride and pretentiousness, nonviolence, forgiveness, uprightness, service of the Master, purity, steadfastenes, self-restraint;

8. Aversion from sense-objects, absence of conceit, realization of the painfulness and evil of birth, death, age and disease;

9. Absence of attachment, refusal to be wrapped up in one's children, wife, home and family, even-mindedness whether good or ill befall;

10. Unwavering and all-exclusive devotion to Me, resort to secluded spots, distaste for the haunts of men;

11. Settled conviction of the nature of the Atman, perception of the goal of the knowledge of Truth,—

All this is declared to be Knowledge and the reverse of it is ignorance.

12. I will (now) expound to thee that which is to be known and knowing which one enjoys immortality; it is the supreme Brahman

which has no beginning, which is called neither Being nor non-Being.

The Supreme can be described neither as Being nor as non-Being. It is beyond definition or description, above all attributes.

13. Everywhere having hands and feet, everywhere having eyes, heads, mouths, everywhere having ears, It abides embracing everything in the universe.

14. Seeming to possess the functions of the senses, It is devoid of all the senses; It touches naught, upholds all; having no gunas, It experiences the gunas.

15. Without all beings, yet within; immovable yet moving, so subtle that It cannot be perceived; so far and yet so near It is.

He who knows It is within It, close to It; mobility and immobility, peace and restlessness, we owe to It, for It has motion and yet is motionless.

16. Undivided, It seems to subsist divided in all beings; this Brahman— That which is to be known as the Sustainer of all, yet It is their Devourer and Creator.

17. Light of all lights, It is said to be beyond darkness; It is knowledge, the object of knowledge, to be gained only by knowledge; It is seated in the hearts of all.

18. Thus have I expounded in brief the Field, Knowledge and That which is to be known; My devotee, when he knows this, is worthy to become one with Me.

19. Know that Prakriti and Purusha are both without beginning; know that all the modifications and gunas are born of Prakriti.

20. Prakriti is described as the cause in the creation of effects from causes; Purusha is described as the cause of the experiencing of pleasure and pain.

21. For the Purusha, residing in Prakriti, experiences the gunas born in Prakriti; attachment to these gunas is the cause of his birth in good or evil wombs.

Prakriti in common parlance is Maya. Purusha is the Jiva. Jiva acting in accordance with his nature experiences the fruit of actions arising out of the three gunas.

22. What is called in this body the Witness, the Assentor, the Sustainer, the Experiencer, the Great Lord and also the Supreme Atman, is Supreme Being.

23. He who thus knows Purusha and Prakriti with its gunas, is not born again, no matter how he live and move.

Read in the light of discourses II, IX and XII this shloka may not be taken to support any kind of libertinism. It shows the virtue of self-surrender and selfless devotion. All actions bind the self, but if all are dedicated to the Lord they do not bind, rather they release him. He who has thus extinguished the 'self or the thought of 'I' and who acts as ever in the great witness' eye, will never sin nor err. the self-sense is at the root of all error or sin. Where the 'I' has ben extinguished, there is no sin. This shloka shows how to steer clear of all sin.

24. Some through meditation hold the Atman by themselves in their own self; others by Sankhya Yoga, and others by Karma Yoga.

25. Yet others, not knowing (Him) thus, worship (Him) having heard from others; they too pass beyond death, because of devoted adherence to what they have heard.

26. Wherever something is born, animate or inanimate, know thou Bharatarshabha, that it issues from the union of the Field and the Knower of the Field.

27. Who sees abiding in all beings the same Parameshvara, imperishable in the perishable, he sees indeed.

28. When he sees the same Ishvara abiding everywhere alike, he does not hurt himself by himself and hence he attains the highest goal.

He who sees the same God everywhere merges in Him and sees naught else; he thus does not yield to passion, does not become his own foe and thus attains Freedom.

29. Who sees that it is Prakriti that performs all actions and thus (knows) that Atman performs them not, he sees indeed.

Just as, in the case of a man who is asleep, his "Self" is not the agent of sleep, but Prakriti, even so the enlightened man will detach his "Self" from all activities. to the pure everything is pure. Prakriti is not unchaste, it is when arrogant man takes her as wife that of these twain passion is born.

30. When he sees the diversity of beings as founded in unity and the whole expanse issuing therefrom, then he attains to Brahman.

To realize that everything rests in Brahman is to attain to the state of Brahman. Then Jiva becomes Shiva.

31. This imperishable Supreme Atman, O Kaunteya, though residing in the body, acts not and is not stained, for he has no beginning and no gunas.

32. As the all-pervading ether, by reason of its subtlety, is not soiled even so Atman pervading every part of the body is not soiled.

33. As the one Sun illumines the whole universe, even so the Master of the Field illumines the whole field, O Bharata!

34. Those who, with the eyes of knowledge, thus perceive the distinction between the Field and the Knower of the Field, and (the secret) of the release o beings from Prakriti, they attain to the Supreme.

Thus ends the thirteenth discourse, entitled 'Kshetra-

kshetrajnavibhaga Yoga' in the converse of Lord Krishna and Arjuna, on the science of Yoga, as part of the knowledge of Brahman in the Upanishad called the Bhagawadgita.

DISCOURCE 14.

The description of Prakriti naturally leads on to that of its constituents, the Gunas, which from the subject of this discourse. And that, in turn, leads to a description of the marks of him who has passed beyond the three gunas. These are practically the same as those of the man of secure understanding (II. 54-72) as also those of the ideal Bhakta (XII. 12-20).

The Lord Said:

1. Yet again I will expound the highest and the best of all knowledge, knowing which all the sages passed hence to the highest perfection.

2. By having recourse to this knowledge they became one with Me. They need not come to birth even at a creation, nor do they suffer at a dissolution.

3. The great prakriti is for me the womb in which I deposit the germ; from it all beings come to birth, O Bharata.

4. Whatever forms take birth in the various species, the great prakriti is their Mother and I the seed-giving Father.

5. Sattva, rajas and tamas are the gunas sprung from prakriti; it is they, O Mahabahu, that keep the imperishable Dweller bound to the body.

6. Of these sattva, being stainless, is light-giving and healing; it binds

with the bond of happiness and the bond of knowledge, O sinless one.

7. Rajas, know thou, is of the nature of passion, the source of thirst and attachment; it keeps man bound with the bond of action.

8. Tamas, know thou, born of ignorance, is mortal man's delusion; it keeps him bound with heedlessness, sloth and slumber, O Bharata.

9. Sattva attaches man to happiness, rajas to action, and tamas, shrouding knowledge, attaches him to heedlessness.

10. Sattva prevails, O Bharata, having overcome rajas and tamas; rajas, when it has overpowered sattva and tamas; likewise tamas reigns when sattva and rajas are crushed.

11. When the light—knowledge—shines forth from al the gates of this body, then it may be known that the sattva thrives.

12. Greed, activity, assumption of undertakings, restlessness, craving— these are in evidence when rajas flourishes, O Bharatarshabha.

13. Ignorance, dullness, heedlessness, and delusion—these are in evidence when tamas reigns, O Kurunandana.

14. If the embodied one meets his end whilst sattva prevails, then he attains to the spotless worlds of the knowers of the Highest.

15. If he dies during the reign within him of rajas, he is born among men attached to action; and if he dies in tamas, he is born in species not endowed with reason.

16. The fruit of sattvika action is said to be stainless merit. That of rajas is pain and that of tamas ignorance.

18. Those abiding in sattva rise upwards, those in rajas stay midway, those in tamas sink downwards.

19. When the seer perceives no agent other than the gunas, and knows Him who is above the gunas, he attains to My being.

As soon as a man realizes that he is not the doer, but the gunas are the agent, the 'self' vanishes, and he goes through all his actions spontaneously, just to sustain the body. And as the body is meant to subserve the highest end, all his actions will even reveal detachment and dispassion. Such a seer can easily have a glimpse of the One who is above the gunas and offer his devotion to Him.

20. When the embodied one transcends these three gunas which are born of his contact with the body, he is released from the pain of birth, death and age and attains deathlessness.

Arjuna Said:

21. What, O Lord, are the marks of him who has transcended the three gunas? How does he conduct himself? How does he transcend the three gunas?

The Lord Said:

22. He, O Pandava, who does not disdain light, activity, and delusion when they come into being, nor desires them when they vanish;

23. He, who seated as one indifferent, is not shaken by the gunas, and stays still and moves not, knowing it is gunas playing their parts;

24. He who holds pleasure and pain alike, who is sedate, who regards as same earth, stone and gold, who is wise and weighs in equal scale things pleasant and unpleasant, who is even-minded in praise and blame;

25. Who holds alike respect and disrespect, who is the same to friend and foe, who indulges in no undertakings—That man is called gunatita.

Shls. 22-25 must be read and considered together. Light activity and delusion, as we have seen in the foregoing shlokas, are the products or indications of sattva, rajas and tamas respectively. The inner meaning of these verses is that he who has transcended the gunas will be unaffected by them. A stone does not desire light, nor does it disdain activity or inertness; it is still, without having the will to be so. If someone puts it into motion, it does not fret; if again, it is allowed to lie still, it does not feel that inertness or delusion has seized it. The difference between a stone and a gunatita is that the latter has full consciousness and with full knowledge he shakes himself free from the bonds that bind an ordinary mortal. He has, as a result of his knowledge, achieved the purpose of a stone. Like the stone he is witness, but not the doer, of the activities of the gunas or prakriti. Of such jnani one may say that he is sitting still, unshaken in the knowledge that it is the gunas playing their parts. We who are every moment of our lives acting as though we are the doers can only imagine the state, we can hardly experience it. But we can hitch our waggon to that star and work our way closer and closer towards it by gradually withdrawing the self from our actions. A gunatita has experience of his own condition but he cannot describe it, for he who can describe it ceases to be one. The moment he proceeds to do so, 'self' peeps in. The peace and light and bustle and inertness of our common experience are illusory. The Gita itself has made it clear in so many words that the sattvika state is the one nearest that of a gunatita. Therefore every one should strive to develop more and more sattva in himself, believing that some day he will reach the goal of the state of gunatita.

26. He who serves me in an unwavering and exclusive bhaktiyoga transcends these gunas and is worthy to become one with Brahman.

27. For I am the very image of Brahman, changeless and deathless, as also of everlasting dharma and perfect bliss.

Thus ends the fourteenth discourse, entitled 'Gunatrayavibhaga Yoga' in the converse of Lord Krishna and Arjuna, on the science of Yoga, as part of the knowledge of Brahman, in the Upanishad called the Bhagawadgita.

DISCOURCE 15.

This discourse deals with the supreme form of the Lord, transcending Kshara (perishable) and Akshara (imperishable).

The Lord Said:

1. With the root above and branches below, the ashvattha tree, they say, is impossible; it has Vedic hymns for its leaves; he who knows it knows the Vedas.

Shvah means tomorrow, and ashvattha (na shvopi sthata) means that which will not last even until tomorrow, i.e. the world of sense which is every moment in a state of flux. But even though it is perpetually changing, as its root is Brahman or the Supreme, it is imperishable. It has for its protection and support the leaves of the Vedic hymns, i.e. dharma. He who knows the world of sense as such and who knows dharma is the real jnani, that man has really known the Vedas.

2. Above all and below its branches spread, blossoming because of the gunas, having for their shoots the sense-objects; deep down in the world of men are ramified its roots, in the shape of the consequences of action.

This is the description of the tree of the world of sense as the unenlightened see it. They fail to discover its Root above in Brahman and so they are always attached to the objects of sense. They water the tree with the three gunas and remain bound to Karman in the world of men.

3. Its form as such is not here perceived, neither is its end, nor beginning, nor basis. Let man first hew down this deep-rooted Ashvattha with the sure weapon of detachment;

4. Let him pray to win to that haven from which there is no return and seek to find refuge in the primal Being from whom has emanated this ancient world of action.

'Detachment in shl. 3 here means dispassion, aversion to the objects of the senses. Unless man is determined to cut himself off from the temptations of the world of sense he will go deeper into the mire every day. These verses show that one dare not play with the objects of the senses with impunity.

5. To that imperishable haven those enlightened souls go—who are without pride and delusion, who have triumphed over the taints of attachment, who are ever in tune with the Supreme, whose passions have died, who are exempt from the pairs of opposites, such as pleasure and pain.

6. Neither the sun, nor the moon, nor fire illumine it; men who arrive there return not—that is My supreme abode.

7. As part indeed of Myself which has been the eternal Jiva in this world of life, attracts the mind and the five senses from their place in prakriti.

8. When the master (of the body) acquires a body and discards it he carries these with him wherever he goes, even as the wind carries scents from flower beds.

9. Having settled himself in the senses—ear, eye, touch, taste, and smell—as well as the mind, through them he frequents their objects.

These objects are the natural objects of the senses. The frequenting or enjoyment of these would be tainted if there were the sense of

'I' about it; otherwise it is pure, even as a child's enjoyment of these objects is innocent.

10. The deluded perceive Him not as He leaves or settles in (a body) or enjoys (sense objects) in association with the gunas; it is those endowed with the eye of knowledge who alone see Him.

11. Yogins who strive see Him seated in themselves; the witless ones who have not cleansed themselves to see Him not, even though they strive.

This does not conflict with the covenant that God has made even with the sinner in discourse 9. Akritatman (who has not cleansed himself) means one who has no devotion in him, who has not made up his mind to purify himself. The most confirmed sinner, if he has humility enough to seek refuge in surrender to God, purifies himself and succeeds in finding Him. Those who do not care to observe the cardinal and the casual vows and expect to find God through bare intellectual exercise are witless, Godless; they will not find Him.

12. The light in the sun which illumines the whole universe and which is in the moon and in fire—that light, know thou, is Mine;

13. It is I, who penetrating the earth uphold all beings with My strength, and becoming the moon—the essence of all sap—nourish all the herbs;

14. It is I who becoming the Vaishvanara Fire and entering the bodies of all that breathe, assimilate the four kinds of food with the help of the outward and the inward breaths.

15. And I am seated in the hearts of all, from Me proceed memory, knowledge and the dispelling of doubts; it is I who am to be known in all the Vedas, I, the author of Vedanta and the knower of the Vedas.

16. There are two Beings in the world: kshara (perishable) and akshara (imperishable). Kshara embraces all creatures and their

permanent basis is akshara.

17. The Supreme Being is surely another—called Paramatman who is the Imperishable Ishvara pervades and supports the three worlds.

18. Because I transcend the kshara and am also higher than the akshara, I am known in the world and in the Vedas as Purushottama (the Highest Being).

19. He who, undeluded, knows Me as Purushottama, knows all, he worships Me with all his heart, O Bharata.

20. Thus I have revealed to thee, sinless one, this most mysterious shastra; he who understands this, O Bharata, is a man of understanding, he has fulfilled his life's mission.

Thus ends the fifteenth discourse, entitled 'purushottama Yoga' in the converse of Lord krishna and Arjuna, on the science of Yoga, as part of the knowledge of Brahman in the Upanishad called the Bhagawadgita.

DISCOURCE 16.

This discourse treats of the divine and the devilish heritage.

The Lord Said:

1. Fearlessness, purity of heart, steadfastness in jnana and yoga—knowledge and action, beneficence, self-restraint, sacrifice, spiritual study, austerity, and uprightness;

2. Non-violence, truth, slowness to wrath, the spirit of dedication, serenity, aversion to slander, tenderness to all that lives, freedom from greed, gentleness, modesty, freedom from levity;

3. Spiritedness, forgiveness, fortitude, purity, freedom from ill-will and arrogance—these are to be found in one born with the divine heritage, O Bharata.

4. Pretentiousness, arrogance, self-conceit, wrath, coarseness, ignorance—these are to be found in one born with the devilish heritage.

5. The divine heritage makes for Freedom, the devilish for bondage. Grieve not, O Partha; thou art born with a divine heritage.

6. There are two orders of created beings in this world—the divine and the devilish; the divine order has been described in detail, hear from Me now of the devilish, O Partha.

7. Men of the devil do not know what they may do and what they may not do; neither is there any purity, nor right conduct, nor truth to be found in them.

8. 'Without truth, without basis, without God is the universe,' they say; 'born of the union of the sexes, prompted by naught but lust.'

9. Holding this view, these depraved souls, of feeble understanding and of fierce deeds, come forth as enemies of the world to destroy it.

10. Given to insatiable lust, possessed by pretentiousness, arrogance and conceit, they seize wicked purposes in their delusion, and go about pledged to uncleaned deeds.

11. Given to boundless cares that end only with their death, making indulgence or lust their sole goal, convinced that that is all;

12. Caught in a myriad snares of hope, slaves to lust and wrath, they speak unlawfully to amass wealth for the satisfaction of their appetites.

13. 'This have I gained today; this aspiration shall I now attain; this wealth is mine; this likewise shall be mine hereafter;

14. 'This enemy I have already slain, others also I shall slay; lord of all am I; enjoyment is mine, perfection is mine, strength is mine, happiness is mine;

15. 'Wealthy am I, and high-born. What other is like unto me? I shall perform a sacrifice! I shall give alms! I shall be merry!' Thus think they, by ignorance deluded;

16. And tossed about by diverse fancies, caught in the net of delusion, stuck deep in the indulgence of appetites, into foul hell they fall.

17. Wise in their own conceit, stubborn, full of the intoxication of pelf and pride, they offer nominal sacrifices for show, contrary to the rule.

18. Given to pride, force, arrogance, lust and wrath they are deriders indeed, scorning Me in their own and other' bodies.

19. These cruel scorners, lowest of mankind and vile, I hurl down again and again, into devilish wombs.

20. Doomed to devilish wombs, these deluded ones, far from ever coming to Me, sink lower and lower in birth after birth.

21. Three-fold is the gate of hell, leading man to perdition—Lust, Wrath, and Greed; these three, therefore, should be shunned.

22. The man who escapes these three gates of Darkness, O Kaunteya, works out his welfare and thence reaches the highest state.

23. He who forsakes the rule of shastra and does but the bidding of his selfish desires, gains neither perfection, nor happiness, nor the highest state.

Shastra does not mean the rites and formulae laid down in the so-called dharmashastra, but the path of self-restraint laid down by the seers and the saints.

24. Therefore let shastra be thy authority for determining what ought to be done and what ought not to be done; ascertain thou the rule of the shastra and do thy task here (accordingly).

Shastra here too has the same meaning as in the preceding shloka. Let no one be a law unto himself, but take as his authority the law laid down by men who have known and lived religion.

Thus ends the sixteenth discourse, entitled 'Daivasurasampadvibhaga Yoga' in the converse of Lord Krishna and Arjuna, on the science of Yoga, as part of the knowledge of Brahman in the Upanishad called the Bhagawadgita.

DISCOURCE 17.

On being asked to consider shastra (conduct of the worthy) as the authority, Arjuna is faced with a difficulty. What is the position of those who may not be able to accept the authority of Shastra but who may act in faith? An answer to the question is attempted in this discourse. Krishna rests content with pointing out the rocks and shoals on the path of the one who forsakes the beaconlight of Shastra (conduct of the worthy). In doing so he deals with the faith and sacrifice, austerity and charity, performed with faith, and their divisions according to the spirit in which they are performed. He also sings the greatness of the mystic syllables AUM TAT SAT—a formula of dedication of all work to God.

Arjuna Said:

1. What, then, O Krishna, is the position of those who forsake the rule of Shastra and yet worship with faith? Do they act from sattva or rajas or tamas?

The Lord Said:

2. Threefold is the faith of men, an expression of their nature in each case; it is sattvika, rajas or tamasa. Hear thou of it.

3. The faith of every man is in accord with his innate character; man is made up of faith; whatever his object of faith, even so is he.

4. Sattvika persons worship the gods; rajas ones, the Yakshas and Rakshasas; and others—men of tamas—worship manes and spirits.

5. Those men who, wedded to pretentiousness and arrogance, possessed by the violence of lust and passion, practice fierce austerity not ordained by shastra;

6. They, whilst they torture the several elements that make up their bodies, torture Me too dwelling in them; know them to be of unholy resolves.

7. Of three kinds again is the food that is dear to each; so also are sacrifice, austerity, and charity. Hear how they differ.

8. Victuals that add to one's years, vitality, strength, health, happiness and appetite; are savoury, rich, substantial and inviting, are dear to the sattvika.

9. Victuals that are bitter, sour, salty, over-hot, spicy, dry, burning, and causing pain, bitterness and disease, are dear to rajasa.

10. Food which has become cold, insipid, putrid, stale, discarded and unfit for sacrifice, is dear to the tamasa.

11. That sacrifice is sattvika which is willingly offered as a duty without desire for fruit and according to the rule.

12. But when sacrifice is offered with an eye to fruit and for vain glory, know, O Bharatashreshtha, that it is rajasa.

13. Sacrifice which is contrary to the rule, which produces no food, which lacks the sacred text, which involves no giving up, which is devoid of faith is said to be tamasa.

14. Homage to the gods, to Brahmanas, to gurus and to wise men; cleanliness, uprightness, brahmacharya and non-violence—these constitute austerity (tapas) of the body.

15. Words that cause no hurt, that are true loving and helpful, and

spiritual study constitute austerity of speech.

16. Serenity, benignity, silence, self-restraint, and purity of the spirit— these constitute austerity of the mind.

17. This threefold austerity practiced in perfect faith by men not desirous of fruit, and disciplined, is said to be sattvika.

18. Austerity which is practiced with an eye to gain praise, honour and homage and for ostentation is said to be rajasa; it is fleeting and unstable.

19. Austerity which is practiced from any foolish obsession, either to torture oneself or to procure another's ruin, is called tamasa.

20. Charity, given as a matter of duty, without expectation of any return, at the right place and time, and to the right person is said to be sattvika.

21. Charity, which is given either in hope of receiving in return, or with a view of winning merit, or grudgingly, is declared to be rajasa.

22. Charity given at the wrong place and time, and to the undeserving recipient disrespectfully and with contempt is declared to be tamasa.

23. AUM TAT SAT has been declared to be the threefold name of Brahman and by that name were created of old the Brahmanas, the Vedas and sacrifices.

24. Therefore, with AUM ever on their lips, are all the rites of sacrifice, charity and austerity, performed always to the rule, by Brahmavadins.

25. With the utterance of TAT and without the desire for fruit are the several rites of sacrifice, austerity and charity performed by those seeking Freedom.

26. SAT is employed in the sense of 'real' and 'good'; O Partha, SAT is also applied to beautiful deeds.

27. Constancy in sacrifice, austerity and charity, is called SAT; and all work for those purposes is also SAT.

The substance of the last four shlokas is that every action should be done in a spirit of complete dedication to God. For AUM alone is the only Reality. That only which is dedicated to It counts.

28. Whatever is done, O Partha, by way of sacrifice, charity or austerity or any other work, is called Asat if done without faith. It counts for naught hereafter as here.

Thus ends the seventeenth discourse, entitled 'Sharaddhatrayavibhaga Yoga' in the converse of Lord Krishna and Arjuna, on the science of Yoga, as part of the knowledge of Brahman in the Upanishad called the Bhagawadgita.

DISCOURCE 18.

This concluding discourse sums up the teaching of the Gita. It may be said to be summed up in the following: "Abandon all duties and come to Me, the only Refuge" (66). That is true renunciation. But abandonment of all duties does not mean abandonment of actions; it means abandonment of the desire for fruit. Even the highest act of service must be dedicated to Him, without the desire. That is Tyaga (abandonment), that is Sannyasa (renunciation).

Arjuna Said:

1. Mahabahu! I would fain learn severally the secret of sannyasa and of tyaga, O Hrishikesha, O Keshinishudana.

The Lord Said:

2. Renunciation of actions springing from selfish desire is known as sannyasa by the seers; abandonment of the fruit of all action is called tyaga by the wise.

3. Some thoughtful persons say: 'All action should be abandoned as an evil'; others say: 'Action for sacrifice, charity and austerity should not be relinquished'.

4. Hear my decision in this matter of tyaga, O Bharatasattama; for tyaga, too, O mightiest of men, has been described to be of three kinds.

5. Action for sacrifice, charity and austerity may not be abandoned; it must needs be performed. Sacrifice, charity and austerity are purifiers of the wise.

6. But even these actions should be performed abandoning all attachment and fruit; such, O Partha, is my best and considered opinion.

7. It is not right to renounce one's allotted task; its abandonment, from delusion, is said to be tamasa.

8. He who abandons action, deeming it painful and for fear of straining his limbs, he will never gain the fruit of abandonment, for his abandonment is rajasa.

9. But when an allotted task is performed from a sense of duty and with abandonment of attachment and fruit, O Arjuna, that abandonment is deemed to be sattvika.

10. Neither does he disdain unpleasant action, nor does he cling to pleasant action—this wise man full of sattva, who practices abandonment, and who has shaken off all doubts.

11. For the embodied one cannot completely abandon action; but he who abandons the fruit of action is named a tyagi.

12. To those who do not practice abandonment accrues, when they pass away, the fruit of action which is of three kinds: disagreeable, agreeable, mixed; but never to the sannyasins.

13. Learn, from me, O Mahabahu, the five factors mentioned in the Sankhyan doctrine for the accomplishment of all action:

14. The field, the doer, the various means, the several different operations, the fifth and the last, the Unseen.

15. Whatever action, right or wrong, a man undertakes to do with the body, speech or mind, these are the five factors thereof.

16. This being so, he who, by reason of unenlightened intellect, sees the unconditioned Atman as the agent—such a man is dense and unseeing.

17. He who is free from all sense of 'I', whose motive is untainted, slays not nor is bound, even though he slay all these worlds.

This shloka though seemingly somewhat baffling is not really so. The Gita on many occasions presents the ideal to attain which the aspirant has to strive but which may not be possible completely to realize in the world. It is like definitions in geometry. A perfect straight line does not exist, but it is necessary to imagine it in order to prove the various propositions. Even so, it is necessary to hold up ideals of this nature as standards for imitation in matters of conduct. This then would seem to be the meaning of this shloka: He who has made ashes of 'self', whose motive is untainted, may slay the whole world, if he will. But in reality he who has annihilated 'self' has annihilated his flesh too, and he whose motive is untainted sees the past, present and future. Such a being can be one and only one—God. He acts and yet is no doer, slays and yet is no slayer. For mortal man and royal road—the conduct of the worthy—is ever before him, viz. ahimsa—holding all life sacred.

18. Knowledge, the object of knowledge, and the knower compose the threefold urge to action; the means, the action and the doer compose the threefold sum of action.

19. Knowledge, action, and the doer are of three kinds according to their different gunas; hear thou these, just as they have been described in the science of the gunas.

20. Know that knowledge whereby one sees in all beings immutable entity—a unity in diversity—to be sattvika.

21. That knowledge which perceives separately in all beings several entities of diverse kinds, know thou to be rajasa.

22. And knowledge which, without reason, clings to one single thing,

as though it were everything, which misses the true essence and is superficial is tamasa.

23. That action is called sattvika which, being one's allotted task, is performed without attachment, without like or dislike, and without a desire for fruit.

24. That action which is prompted by the desire for fruit, or by the thought of 'I', and which involves much dissipation of energy is called rajasa.

25. That action which is blindly undertaken without any regard to capacity and consequences, involving loss and hurt, is called tamasa.

26. That doer is called sattvika who has shed all attachment, all thought of 'I', who is filled with firmness and zeal, and who recks neither success nor failure.

27. That doer is said to be rajasa who is passionate, desirous of the fruit of action, greedy, violent, unclean, and moved by joy and sorrow.

28. That doer is called tamasa who is undisciplined, vulgar, stubborn, knavish, spiteful, indolent, woebegone, and dilatory.

29. Hear now, O Dhananjaya, detailed fully and severally, the threefold division of understanding and will, according to their gunas.

30. That understanding, O Partha, is sattvika which knows action from inaction, what ought to be done from what ought not to be done, fear from fearlessness and bondage from release.

31. That understanding, O Partha, is rajasa, which decides erroneously between right and wrong, between what ought to be done and what ought not to be done.

32. That understanding, O Partha, is tamasa, which, shrouded in darkness, thinks wrong to be right and mistakes everything for its reverse.

33. That will, O Partha, is sattvika which maintains an unbroken harmony between the activities of the mind, the vital energies and the senses.

34. That will, O Partha, is rajasa which clings, with attachment, to righteousness, desire and wealth, desirous of fruit in each case.

35. That will, O Partha, is tamasa, whereby insensate man does not abandon sleep, fear, grief, despair and self-conceit.

36. Hear now from Me, O Bharatarshabha, the three kinds of pleasure.

Pleasure which is enjoyed only by repeated practice, and which puts an end to pain,

37. Which, in its inception, is as poison, but in the end as nectar, born of the serene realization of the true nature of Atman—that pleasure is said to be sattvika.

38. That pleasure is called rajasa which, arising from the contact of the senses with their objects, is at first as nectar but in the end like poison.

39. That pleasure is called tamasa which arising from sleep and sloth and heedlessness, stupefies the soul both at first and in the end.

40. There is no being, either on earth or in heaven among the gods, that can be free from these three gunas born of prakriti.

41. The duties of Brahmanas, Kshatriyas, Vaishyas, and Shudras, are distributed according to their innate qualifications, O Parantapa.

42. Serenity, self-restraint, austerity, purity, forgiveness, uprightness, knowledge and discriminative knowledge, faith in God are the Brahmana's natural duties.

43. Valour, spiritedness, constancy, resourcefulness, not fleeing from battle, generosity, and the capacity to rule are the natural duties of

a Kshatriya.

44. Tilling the soil, protection of the cow and commerce are the natural functions of a Vaishya, while service is the natural duty of a Shudra.

45. Each man, by complete absorption in the performance of his duty, wins perfection. Hear now how he wins such perfection by devotion to that duty.

46. By offering the worship of his duty to Him who is the moving spirit of all beings, and by whom all this is pervaded, man wins perfection.

47. Better one's own duty, though uninviting, than another's which may be more easily performed; doing duty which accords with one's nature, one incurs no sin.

The central teaching of the Gita is detachment—abandonment of the fruit of action. And there would be no room for this abandonment if one were to prefer another's duty to one's own. Therefore one's own duty is said to be better than another's. It is the spirit in which duty is done that matters, and its unattached performance is its own reward.

48. One should not abandon, O Kaunteya, that duty to which one is born, imperfect though it be; for all action, in its inception, is enveloped in imperfection, as fire in smoke.

49. He who has weaned himself of all kinds, who is master of himself, who is dead to desire, attains through renunciation the perfection of freedom from action.

50. Learn now from Me, in brief, O Kaunteya, how he who has gained this perfection, attains to Brahman, the supreme consummation of knowledge.

51. Equipped with purified understanding, restraining the self with

firm will, abandoning sound and other objects of the senses, putting aside likes and dislikes,

52. Living in solitude, spare in diet, restrained in speech, body and mind, ever absorbed in dhyanayoga, anchored in dispassion,

53. Without pride, violence, arrogance, lust, wrath, possession, having shed all sense of 'mine' and at peace with himself, he is fit to become one with Brahman.

54. One with Brahman and at peace with himself, he grieves not, nor desires; holding all beings alike, he achieves supreme devotion to Me.

55. By devotion, he realizes in truth how great I am, who I am; and having known Me in reality he enters into Me.

56. Even whilst always performing actions, he who makes Me his refuge wins, by My grace, the eternal and imperishable haven.

57. Casting, with thy mind, all actions on Me, make Me thy goal, and resorting to the yoga of even-mindedness fix thy thought ever on Me.

58. Fixing his thy thought on Me, thou shalt surmount all obstacles by My grace; but if possessed by the sense of 'I' thou listen not, thou shalt perish.

59. If obsessed by the sense of 'I', thou thinkest, 'I will not fight', vain is thy obsession; (thy) nature will compel thee.

60. What thou wilt not do, O Kaunteya, because of thy delusion, thou shalt do, even against thy will, bound as thou art by the duty to which thou art born.

61. God, O Arjuna, dwells in the heart of every being and by His delusive mystery whirls them all, (as though) set on a machine.

62. In Him alone seek thy refuge with all thy heart, O Bharata. By

His grace shalt thou win to the eternal haven of supreme peace.

63. Thus have I expounded to thee the most mysterious of all knowledge; ponder over it fully, then act as thou wilt.

64. Hear again My supreme word, the most mysterious of all; dearly beloved thou art of Me, hence I desire to declare thy welfare.

65. On Me fix thy mind, to Me bring thy devotion, to Me offer thy sacrifice, to Me make thy obeisance; to Me indeed shalt thou come—solemn is My promise to thee, thou art dear to Me.

66. Abandon all duties and come to Me the only refuge. I will release thee from all sins; grieve not!

67. Utter this never to him who knows no austerity, has no devotion, nor any desire to listen, nor yet to him who scoffs at Me.

68. He who will propound this supreme mystery to My devotees, shall, by that act of highest devotion to Me, surely come to Me.

69. Nor among men is there any who renders dearer service to Me than he; nor shall there be on earth any more beloved by Me than he.

It is only he who has himself gained the knowledge and lived it in his life that can declare it to others. These two shlokas cannot possibly have any reference to him, who no matter how he conducts himself, can give flawless reading and interpretation of the Gita.

70. And the man of faith who, scorning not, will but listen to it,—even he shall be released and will go to the happy worlds of men of virtuous deeds.

72. Hast thou heard this, O Partha, with a concentrated mind? Has thy delusion, born of ignorance, been destroyed, O Dhananjaya?

Arjuna Said:

73. Thanks to Thy grace, O Achyuta, my delusion is destroyed, my understanding has returned. I stand secure, my doubts all dispelled; I will do thy bidding.

Sanjaya Said:

74. Thus did I hear this marvellous and thrilling discourse between Vasudeva and the great-souled Partha.

75. It was by Vyasa's favor that I listened to this supreme and mysterious Yoga as expounded by the lips of the Master of Yoga, Krishna Himself.

76. O King, as often as I recall that marvellous and purifying discourse between Keshava and Arjuna, I am filled with recurring rapture.

77. And as often as I recall that marvellous form of Hari, my wonder knows no bounds and I rejoice again and again.

78. Wheresoever Krishna, the Master of Yoga, is, and wheresoever is Partha the Bowman, there rest assured are Fortune, Victory, Prosperity, and Eternal Right.

Thus ends the eighteenth discourse, entitled 'Sannyasa Yoga' in the converse of Lord Krishna and Arjuna, on the science of Yoga, as part of the knowledge of Brahman in the Upanishad called the Bhagawadgita.

तस्मादसक्तः सततं कार्यं कर्म समाचर।
असक्तो ह्याचरन्कर्म परमाप्नोति पूरुषः।।

tasmādasaktah satatam kāryaṁ karma samācara,
asakto hyācarankarma paramāpnoti pūruṣaḥ.